LOVING OUR KIDS
ON PURPOSE

LOVING OUR KIDS ON PURPOSE

Making a Heart-to-Heart Connection

DANNY SILK

DESTINY IMAGE® PUBLISHERS, INC.
P.O. Box 310, Shippensburg, PA 17257-0310
"Promoting Inspired Lives."

This book and all other Destiny Image, Revival Press, MercyPlace, Fresh Bread, Destiny Image Fiction, and Treasure House books are available at Christian bookstores and distributors worldwide.

This book is a re-release of *Loving Our Kids on Purpose*, 13-digit ISBN: 978-0-7684-2739-4, copyright 2008.

For a U.S. bookstore nearest you, call 1-800-722-6774.
For more information on foreign distributors, call 717-532-3040.
Reach us on the Internet: www.destinyimage.com.

ISBN 10: 0-7684-0352-9
ISBN 13 TP: 978-0-7684-0352-7
ISBN 13 EBook: 978-0-7684-8482-3

For Worldwide Distribution, Printed in the U.S.A.

6 / 15

DEDICATION PAGE

This book is dedicated to my children: my oldest child, Brittney, and her husband, Ben; my oldest son, Levi; and my funniest child, Taylor. You have all brought out the best in me. I love you, completely, with all my heart.

ACKNOWLEDGMENTS

My Chosen, Sheri: You've helped me become the man I always hoped I would become. I love you!

Bill and Beni Johnson: There is no one on this planet who has so completely restructured my internal world and impacted my legacy as have the two of you. Thank you!

Kris and Kathy Vallotton: Who does the counselor go to when his marriage is in trouble? Best friends. Thank you for always being there for us.

John and Sandy Tillery: You imparted into my life my love for community and service. You taught me that there is no such thing as "secular." You showed me how big life's adventure becomes when I pour my life out for the whole world. Thank you!

Mountain Chapel, Weaverville, California: You took a boy and made a man out of him. Thank you!

Bethel Church, Redding, California: You've taken that man and are changing the world with him. Thank you for sending me all over the globe.

Allison Armerding: You are making me look like a genius. Thanks!

ENDORSEMENTS

It is very difficult to promote Danny Silk's ministry without sounding like I have the need to exaggerate. But the truth is, in the circle I run in, he is without equal. His discernment gives him access to root issues that have become obstacles to relational peace and blessing, while his wisdom enables him to be a "builder of families" and an "architect of relationships." I heartily recommend Danny and all his materials to help bring about God's best for your life.

—Bill Johnson
Senior Leader, Bethel Church
Redding, California

I have known Danny Silk for more then 25 years. He has the most amazing ability to understand the root causes of social and behavioral issues of anyone I have ever encountered in my 30 years of working with people. Our team has been encouraging him to write this book for a long time, as his timeless wisdom needs to be imparted to the masses.

But reader beware: Danny's insights often smash old religious mindsets and free people from the bondage of spiritual captivity. You will find that you are laughing and crying yourself into new relational paradigms as you willingly walk headfirst into his sword. His stories will capture your heart; his wisdom will astonish you; and his life will change you forever. This book is a must read for everyone, whether you have children or not.

—Kris Vallotton
Senior Associate Pastor of Bethel Church
Cofounder of the Bethel School of Supernatural Ministry
Author of *The Supernatural Ways of Royalty* and
Developing a Supernatural Lifestyle

As a high school principal, I had the privilege of watching Danny Silk in action with both my staff and parents. When Danny and I first met, I was at my wits' end, having grown tired of giving advice to hurting parents who treated the symptoms of broken relationships yet ignored the diseases that caused them. *Loving Our Kids on Purpose* is a powerful tool that describes the *why,* but also gives honest, practical application as to *how* we should raise our children in a loving environment that will allow their destinies to come forth. Parenting is the greatest call on our lives, as well as the most difficult task we could ever face. Danny's honesty and ability to tell stories that every parent can relate to shows, through example, how God's New Covenant with us applies to parenting and allows us to nurture a right relationship with our children through love, instead of fear.

I have seen it work firsthand in my school, where parents and children reconnected their hearts and the fruits of love and peace became evident in their lives. This book is a must-read for every parent, teacher, social worker, or anyone who is connected to kids and families. Danny's revelations are tools for success in achieving our most important goal—raising children to fulfill the destiny God has for them.

—Chris Adams
Administrator of Educational Services
Shasta Union High School District
Redding, California

My friend Danny Silk has at last brought his insights and giftings for effective and healthy parenting toward the goal of strong, functional families to print. With the profoundly biblical theme of child rearing majoring on the issues and connections of the heart, Danny presents a challenging example of how the Kingdom of God is the kingdom of right relationships.

Ultimately, Danny demonstrates convincingly that we parents are responsible for building and nurturing home environments of love, respect, honor, and liberty, unsoiled by fear, control, perfectionism, and overreaction to mistakes. Danny guides us systematically through how providing a framework of acceptable choices and fostering internal discipline in our children—teaching them to own their problems in order to champion solutions—results in the building of their Christian character. Danny offers blueprints equipping us with parenting tools with purpose: disciplining for attitude and relationship instead of the distraction of chasing behaviors; favoring love and heart-connection over rules and mindless compliance; and training our children to navigate the waters of freedom and opportunity through the responsible sharing of power and control, lest they grow up strangers to such and thereby become easy prey for a world awash in bad options.

—André Van Mol, MD
Family Physician

Danny Silk is passionate about helping families reach their highest potential in loving communications. He is an innovative and hilarious speaker, teaching God's truths about love, honor, and respect in an easily digestible fashion to both Christian and secular audiences. Sheri, his equally wise and funny wife, often joins him in conference and seminar presentations, a two-for-one dynamic duo.

I have been a counselor for 40 years and continue to glean new revelations about healthy family interactions each time I hear Danny present. He has shared locally, nationally, and inter-nationally in churches, schools, and community settings. His material and appearances are not to be missed.

—Kay Morris Long, M.S.W.
Licensed Clinical Social Worker

Danny Silk is an amazing pastor and a wise teacher, but above all, he has been an incredible friend to me. I can proudly say that he has been one of the most impacting people in my life, mainly due to the fact that his concepts of love, honor, respect, and free-dom are not just the subject he teaches but the way he lives.

Transformation looks to be his favorite word. And I have learned from him how to get out from fear and control-based relationships into real love and freedom. Even my marriage, my family, and my whole church have been transformed.

I am sure that *Loving Our Kids on Purpose* will bring a tremendous insight to the reader about not just how to raise kids, but also how to relate to each other. But the main things in this book are truths that will allow you to raise a generation of free and powerful children—something we really need in this world.

Loving Our Kids on Purpose is a book that every parent, teacher, and pastor should read.

—Angel Nava
Senior Pastor
Seeds of Life Church (Semillas de Vida)
La Paz, Mexico

As I was reading this, I realized (again) that what I thought was radical protection was actually my need to control every situation with my own children. These principles give me the opportunity to have a relationship with my children that is based in love, not control.

Once I started reading, I couldn't put it down!

—Debra Reed
Director of Children's Ministries
Bethel Church, Redding, California

There is no amount of prescriptions, behavior contracts, or juvenile detention centers that will ever take the place of *Loving Our Kids on Purpose*. Thank you, Danny Silk, for giving us a practical guide to bringing God's perfect love to our youth. If we as a Christian community cannot connect with our youth in a meaningful and loving way—all is lost. Treat youth as problems, and they will become problems. Treat them as children of God, and the fruits will be seen for decades to come.

—Christine M. Lewin, EdD
High School District Administrator

Danny Silk is an outstanding teacher and storyteller. You will laugh and be pleasantly surprised as Danny opens your eyes to a unique perspective of bringing God's love as the overriding attitude for parenting and disciplining your children. You will receive specific tools as well as copious illustrations to bring home the attitudes and concepts that God has taught Danny through his own personal journey of parenting. The greatest benefit of all is that you will hear over and over of the goodness of God and how to view family relationships through the eyes of His love.

—Barry Byrne, MS
Licensed Marriage & Family Therapist
President, Living Strong, Inc.

Loving Our Kids on Purpose has been life giving to our family. It has brought peace into parenting. It is the handbook children should come with.

—Anthony and Jenney Mason—Parents of three

Danny has greatly impacted our culture. COMPASS Care Services employs over 120 individuals, and his trainings have given our team a clear understanding of values such as personal freedom and responsibility. Our supervisors have received powerful tools for communicating esteem to their subordinates, while still holding them accountable for their choices. Our employees were so touched by his concepts and messages, they are still using "Dannyisms" three months later! We are going to have him back again and again, to further mine his wisdom and expertise.

—Eric Hess
CEO COMPASS Care Services
Dublin, California

As a single mom and business owner, you could say I have some stress in my life. I am so grateful to Danny and this book: My home has gone from a place of chaos and confusion, to a place of peace and love. I am daily implementing *everything* I have learned from this material and have gone from anger and grief-filled relationships with my children to fun, loving, heart-connected relationships. I never thought I could really be "in love" with my sons because of all the rage and anger I carried. It brings tears to my eyes when I look back at where we were and where we are today.

—Dina Gifford—Mother of three

I love this parenting style; our children are already becoming very "fun to be with" and making amazing choices. I can take them anywhere with me with no hassles or frustrations. I actually enjoy shopping with my kids. I always get great reports when Aiden goes to friends' houses to play, as he is becoming a fabulous decision maker even at 4 years old. He loves to report to me the good decisions he makes, and he is very proud when he makes fun-to-be-with choices. Thanks, Danny, for all your wonderful insight, knowledge, and help.

—Christie Farrelly—Mother of three

While getting my daughter ready for school last week, I yelled "Hurry up!" To which my almost-3-year-old replied, "You're not bein' very fun da be with, Mom." In that very moment, I realized—it's working.

—Jenn Johnson—Mother of three

Loving Our Kids on Purpose brought our very different parenting styles (each built from our very different family life experiences) from a "his way/her way" approach. Now, we just have "our way." What a joy to be working from the same playbook.

We have gone through the series repeatedly, both together and separately. Funny thing about these tools—the principles work on all ages, so be prepared to have a more healthy relationship with everyone around you!

—Aaron and Krisann Gentry—New parents

What I love about my children is the tremendous value they have for themselves. In their minds, all adults should have the same tremendous value for them! I attribute this to *Loving Our Kids on Purpose* and having Danny and Sheri Silk in our lives!

—Anna Ladd—Mother of three

I am so thankful for the tools and principles taught in *Loving Our Kids on Purpose*. Beyond the great techniques, I love the mindset that promotes a safe environment for my children to learn and grow now in order for them to make wise choices for the rest of their lives. Thank you for providing a way to train my children with respect and honor; it's invaluable!

—Jerome and Amanda Evans—Parents of two

After beginning our marriage as "second timers," my husband and I had a lot of cleaning up to do in the parenting department. Several years (and children!) later, we can see the fruit of *Loving Our Kids on Purpose* in our daily connections with each other and each one of our children. From the 3-year-old to the 23-year-old, we have been able to establish relationships that are driven by a desire for connection and not by the "his, hers, and ours" calamity that befalls so many combined families.

—Eric and Angela Brooks—Parents of seven

The principles of *Loving Our Kids on Purpose* have brought peace into our parenting style. It has made parenting a joy and being with our kids fun.

—Ian and Jennifer Kilpatrick—Parents of four

Last week my 8-year-old daughter, Maci, was refusing to get dressed for school and having a tantrum. I told her that was fine if she didn't want to get dressed, but if she wasn't dressed by 8:08 A.M., I was taking her to school in her jammies. She immediately stopped her tantrum, got dressed, and was in the car ready to go! Thanks, Danny, for all of your wisdom and help in parenting! We love you, and so does Maci!

—Heather Ferrante—Mother of two

This style of parenting is all about freedom. Learning how to let your children think for themselves and take control and responsibility for their own choices is very freeing as a parent. Through it, I have learned how truly *amazing* and capable my children are!

—Christine Boring—Mother of two

There are moments as a parent that you wonder, "Am I doing it right?" *Loving Our Kids on Purpose* gives the tools and confidence that makes you feel like the genius and you look at your kids and realize, they are truly Kingdom Giants. Thank you, Danny and Sheri.

—Scott and Julie Pewitt—Parents of three

Loving Our Kids on Purpose is training us, as parents, to build a loving connection with our children that will carry us through the teen years and beyond. Teaching our children to make good choices and operate in self-control at a young age is one of the greatest gifts we can give them, and *Loving Our Kids On Purpose* is teaching us how to do just that.

—Peter and Jennifer Johnston—Parents of three

As grandparents, we are using your teaching, too. Our kids are implementing the principles with their kids, and so we are trying to carry over when we are with Judah and Jaron. Wish we could have had these principles when we were raising our kids.

—Jeff and Cathy Sampson—Grandparents to two boys

TABLE OF CONTENTS

FOREWORD

For as long as I can remember, I have considered being a parent to be the ultimate privilege in life. There is nothing that compares to that honor. Think about it: God actually entrusts us with the life of another human being to raise for His purposes. If that is true, then raising children for God is the ultimate responsibility in life.

When my wife and I started to have children—and we have three—we had many well-meaning people warn us of the coming difficulties we'd have while they grew up. They say, "He's really cute right now. But just wait until he's two!" They called it the *terrible twos*. And then it was, "Just wait until they go to school," or the more popular, "Just wait until they're teenagers." It seemed like everyone wanted to warn us of potential problems, but no one told us the answers to the issues. It almost felt like those who had trouble raising their children seemed to be hoping we would have trouble, too, so they could feel better about their experience. We were young and naïve—who were we to think we could do any better?

Beni and I decided early on to ignore such warnings, cleanse them from our minds, and approach the privilege of raising children as a divine assignment for which He had given us all the tools we'd need to do it well. We watched as each season in our children's lives brought new challenges where divine wisdom was needed. But we also found that God was eager to impart His wisdom to us. Every season was unique and wonderful. We celebrated life, wept at failure, and approached every step with great hope and purpose. The resolve we made at the beginning held true. Our three children are now happily married with children of their own, and grandchildren are now on our radar. And each season really is better than the former.

Now we frequently tell parents that each age is fun, and it just gets better and better. We've had many thank us just for giving them hope, because apparently those who warned us of our coming crises in parenting have reproduced after their kind, spreading their fear and terror to young parents, thinking they are doing them a favor. We must reverse this mindset. It should not exist in the church!

Although it is no secret that the family has been in crisis, it is also known that the restoration of the family is high on God's list of priorities. That means that Heaven is banking on our success. But how? That's where Danny Silk comes into the picture with *Loving Our Kids on Purpose*. He has given me hope that such an insurmountable task of seeing the family restored nationwide is actually possible.

It is so difficult to describe the depth and profound nature of this book. Danny's wisdom is extremely rare. Yes, it's about raising children. And yes, tools are given to do it well. But the overwhelming nature of this book is that it gives us wisdom, vision, and purpose to be able to shape the course of world history. It's true. Danny sets the big picture so firmly in place that you cannot forget it. The core values of the Kingdom of God, a kingdom of liberty, become the bedrock of the family—your family.

Jesus said that the Kingdom of God is within us. That means that all Kingdom issues are heart issues. That is Danny's area of expertise: the heart. He effectively cuts to the quick of the issues of life, enabling each parent to make necessary corrections to restore purpose and joy to the parenting experience. You'll laugh, cry, and most likely repent as you read this book. And each expression is welcomed in our quest to impact the world through Kingdom families.

I've had the privilege of working with Danny for many years. I've watched as, through his influence, families with multigenerational disasters get reversed in weeks, not years. The impact on our community is astounding. This book is so profound I wish I could make it required reading by all believers, not just parents. It is about heart, Kingdom, and our eternal purpose. Enjoy!

—Bill Johnson

PREFACE

I have been teaching parenting education since 1991. It all started when I began a quest to find a method for instructing Christian foster parents to discipline children without the use of corporal punishment. I'd never considered how much of parenting involved spanking, or at least the threat of spanking, until that quest. Sheri and I had spanked our first child, Brittney, without a thought to what we might do otherwise. Meanwhile, most of the families I recruited as new foster parents were of the same paradigm.

One day, while visiting a foster/adoptive home of a veteran foster parent, I observed something I'd never seen before. She had nine children in her home. Some were adopted already and the others were foster children. Most of the foster children were in line for adoption by this lady. All these children were diagnosed Reactive Attachment Disorder (RAD). This is a severe condition in which children cannot bond with caregivers and often cannot bond at all with other people. Several of these children had done such extreme acting out behaviors that they were removed from their biological parents at early ages. Burning the family home to the ground, strangling siblings, killing family pets, and violence against parents are just a few of the things her foster children had done before coming to her home.

I had no idea of any of this prior to my arrival at her house. As I entered her environment, I noticed children quietly sitting in places arranged around the home. She was home schooling all of these children. Well-behaved, self-controlled children were all I could see. She told me of some of the bizarre events that had taken place at her home. She described behaviors that would end placement in most foster homes. Instead, this woman was adding these kinds of children to her home.

I asked how on earth she was doing this. And this was when everything began to shift in my thinking and behavior toward my world. She mentioned to me that she had connected with a center in Golden, Colorado, called the Cline-Fay Institute. It was there that she received help with her first adoptive son, who was diagnosed RAD. This center specialized in creating a bond between severely abused children and their caregivers and parents. She then explained to me something called *Love and Logic*®.

This was the first I'd ever heard of *Love and Logic*, but it had been around for many years. She had a catalog and I ordered two cassette tapes: "The 4 Steps to Responsibility" and "Helicopters, Drill Sergeants, and Consultants." I listened to these two cassettes for a year in my car. They were full of fun stories that helped me catch the principles and remember the steps of how to use the skills.

I started sharing *Love and Logic* with my foster parents and soon began doing parenting education training for them. Eventually, the company I worked for, Remi Vista, ordered a training curriculum for parents and I reviewed it. It was going to take too long to do it their way, so I revised it and began teaching it to our foster parents. Within two years, I was teaching a six-hour *Love and Logic*–type seminar in schools and parent groups all over our county. I never looked back.

Foster Cline and Jim Fay, the creators of Love and Logic®, had put into words and skills what I knew was a pattern after God's own heart. The foundation of everything in this book comes from my years of training parents and living it out myself in the context of my faith. Though I have never met these men, I am eternally grateful for their influence in my life and the lives of those I now influence. Peace!

Introduction

Welcome to *Loving Our Kids on Purpose!* This may or may not be new information to you, but it is most likely a radical paradigm shift. This book will challenge what you've come to know as love, discipline, honor, and your overall goal of parenting. As well, this book will introduce you to a way of thinking and living that will bring an ease and peace to your family and other relationships.

This book is going to change the quality of life in your home. No more arguments with your children. That's right! No more fights over whether it is "fair" or "right." Say good-bye to fights about getting homework done or chores finished on time. You can get control of your life back and learn to watch your children through a new set of eyes.

You are going to be set on a course that will show your children the heart of God like never before. You will come to know the peace and joy that you have always wanted as a parent. You are going to learn how "Love drives out fear." This book is going to show you how to build a loving, trusting relationship with your children that inspires them to take care of your heart while they are out making their own decisions about life. Yes, this book will help you learn to trust your children.

We are going to explore how powerful your children were designed to be. You will be amazed at how responsible, respectful, and self-controlled your kids can be. Although this will not happen in a snap of the fingers, you will be able to try things while you read the book and experience immediate results.

As with any new paradigm shift, you will need to import a steady supply of reinforcement concerning what you are learning. Therefore, we have six hours of recorded workshops that you can order from the lovingonpurpose.com Website. In addition, MP3s, CDs, DVDs, and workbook manuals are available to keep your momentum building. I understand that if this is your first exposure to this approach to parenting, you will need some "processing" time and some victories before you can redirect your entire way of living as a family. I highly recommend that you get the supportive training materials to build on what is presented to you in this book. Support materials are also available from *Love and Logic*® at www.loveandlogic.com.

I hope you enjoy reading this first work of mine.

Chapter 1

THE HEART OF THE MATTER

In the autumn of 2006, my friend Banning Liebscher (the youth pastor of Bethel Church) and I had the opportunity to present a parenting series derived from *Becoming a Love and Logic Parent*®. We had six weeks of weekly two-hour meetings with parents who had freshmen students in danger of being expelled from the school. Poor attendance, failing grades, and referrals to the office for discipline earmarked families for this program. Although the program had been aggressively promoted, it was still voluntary, and only four parents attended the first night. Fortunately, several other families from the community had heard about the training and came as well, helping to fill the room.

A woman, who seemed guarded and "hard," was sitting on the front row as I taught and interacted with the group. It turned out that she was overwhelmed and hurting. She finally got to the point where she had enough of me talking as though parenting issues were easy to deal with and blurted out, in both frustration and hope, "Ok, Mr. Know-It-All! I have a 14-year-old girl who fights with me at least five times a day. She fights with her brother and sister whenever she is around them. She is failing all her classes, smoking pot, sleeping with her boyfriend, and sneaking out of the house at night. What are you going to do about that, huh?"

The room was stunned. Everyone in the room had his or her own story, but this lady's was clearly the most desperate. She was completely worn out. Her oldest child was out of control, and her home was in absolute chaos.

I just looked at her, nodding my head and trying to shake off having been called "Mr. Know-It-All." Finally, I said, "Tell me about your connection with your daughter. Describe the heart-to-heart connection between the two of you."

She looked at me with eyes that asked, "What?" So I repeated what I had said. She was not expecting that response. No one in the room was expecting it. We all sat in silence as she thought for a few minutes and then came the tears. This mother put her head down and said, "We do not have a connection. We are scared of each other."

I said, "This is the biggest problem that you have right now with your girl. This disconnection is the culprit. We need a solution to this problem before we can ever approach solutions to the other issues."

She looked at me like I had popped her on the nose with a rolled-up newspaper. She couldn't believe what she was hearing. She thought she needed a more effective way of controlling her daughter and knew that nothing she had tried so far was working. It had been a long time since she'd thought about their love.

We talked briefly about some ways to repair their connection, and off she went. The next week, I asked if anyone had tried anything new in the last week and if there were any questions I might answer before we started the next segment. Still sitting in the front row, but now smiling, the woman said, "It's a miracle! We only fought twice this week! It's a miracle! She is kinder to everyone in the house. We are all in shock. It's a miracle!"

The room erupted in applause. She beamed with hope and victory.

I asked her what she had done. Her response was priceless.

"I went home thinking about what you said about our connection. I'd never even considered that was the problem. I then realized that I wasn't being myself anymore in our relationship. I was hurt and angry all the time toward her. I was more of a control freak than ever. I had no idea that I was as much a part of this problem as she was. So, I did what you said and cleaned up my mess. I apologized for being controlling and disrespectful. I told her that things were going to be different because I was going to change. I told her that I loved her more than she could ever imagine. I cried and held her." She giggled while telling the story. "I think I scared the crap out of her."

That was week three. The following week, this mom came into class and her daughter walked in behind her. She didn't make eye contact with me and chose a seat at the top of the theater-style seating in the room. All by herself, she sat there looking down on the sparsely occupied room.

Her mom had another testimony that night for the class. She said, "We didn't fight at all this week. That hasn't happened in years." She was beaming and bouncing up and down in her chair, clapping for herself. She then turned and pointed to the young lady at the top row of seats. "My daughter came to class with me tonight to find out what you guys are doing to her mother."

The class erupted into laughter and applause.

The following week the mother came to class trailed by her daughter and her other two kids. All of them sat through the class on the front row working on homework next to their mom.

On the sixth and final week, I asked the same question I had asked the previous weeks: "Are there any questions or situations that you need help with?" The class had a response that Banning and I, who have subsequently led these meetings two or three times a year for three years at this high school, have found to be common. First, there was an eerie silence. Then finally, one of the parents said, "I don't know what is happening in other homes, but in our home there is peace."

THE BOTTOM LINE

Do your family relationships manifest the fruit of peace? Isaiah 9:7 declares: "There will be no end to the increase of His government or of peace..." (NASB). Peace is a fruit of the Kingdom of God. But how do you establish the government of Heaven in your home? In order to answer this question, you will have to examine your "bottom line." What is the most important issue for you as a parent when you are interacting with your children? Does the motivating factor in your parenting match up with what drives the Father's heart toward His children? Recognizing your bottom line is truly the first task at hand.

I would submit that for most of us parents, the goal of raising children is to teach them to *obey*. From the time we meet them at birth, our efforts are directed toward shaping the wills and wants of our children. We show them what is "good" and "bad" and then teach them to choose "good." With all our might, we try to ensure that they turn out "good," and the obvious method for accomplishing this goal is to teach them to *do as we say*.

This book will show you that the goal of obedience and compliance is an inferior goal. It can actually be detrimental to both your children's development of personal responsibility and their perception of God the Father. Although obedience is an important part of our relationship with our children, it is not the most important quality. If we fail to take care of the most important matters first, what we build on top of our foundation will not support what we were hoping to accomplish as parents.

When the Pharisees asked Jesus what the most important commandment was, He startled them with His response. They were trying to trap him with His answer, but instead of painting Himself into a corner, He opened up a revelation to them. His response was, in essence, "Love God, love your neighbor, and love yourself" (Luke 10:27). The greatest commandment is *love*. These Pharisees had hoped that He was going to say, "Obey *this* commandment," because their culture was steeped in the priority of obedience and compliance to "the rules." In one fell swoop, Jesus promoted *relationship* above the *rules*. Love and relationship are the bottom line of the Kingdom, and they must be ours if we wish to establish a Kingdom culture in our homes.

There is a huge difference between a culture where obedience and compliance are the bottom line and a culture where relationship is the bottom line. The contrast is perhaps seen most clearly when people fail. Imagine this: Your sixth grader comes to you with his report card, which reveals a failing grade. How do you think you would respond (or how have you responded) to such a scenario? For most parents, their immediate attention is on the child's lack of compliance with his school environment and/or their parental expectations. They work to set their child on a path back to a *good student* position by communicating their disappointment (and often their anger) and giving instructions on how to behave better.

There is really nothing wrong with this approach to dealing with the problem in general. But it perpetuates a problem if the parents are using it to reach an inferior goal, because it never really addresses the heart issues that lead to mistakes in the first place, and it doesn't help parents to stay aware of their own hearts. Until our children learn to deal with what is going on inside of them, they simply cannot learn to manage *freedom*.

I want to propose to you that freedom is a top priority in Heaven, because it is what makes relationships possible. Heaven's culture of relationships is vastly different than most everything we see on earth because God, the Father, is less interested in compliance and much more interested in love. This is the reason that He is trying to prepare us to *live absolutely free lives in an environment of unlimited options* more than trying to keep us from sin. This is the heart of *Loving Our Kids on Purpose,* and so I would like to show you how to love your own kids with this goal in mind.

OUR STORY

My wife, Sheri, and I have been parents for over 20 years now, and I can say that raising three children has been one of the greatest joys I have ever experienced in my life, and probably the greatest challenge. The main part of that challenge for both of us has been learning to parent our children in a way that is completely foreign to the way that we ourselves were parented. Having children confronted us like never before with the fact that we could not afford to continue to use and give away as an inheritance the tools our parents had given us for life.

In fact, let me take you back to a time long, long ago. In a day when dinosaurs roamed the earth—OK, no, not quite that far back—there were two young people named Danny and Sheri. These two, not too long after becoming Christians and getting married, were given the gift of a precious little child, and they named her Brittney. Now, these two people didn't have Clue #1 on how to raise a child, but that has never been one of the qualifiers for having one. You see, in California, anyone can have a child. It is as easy as going fishing, except there is no license required, there are no seasons when you can or cannot have a child, and there is no limit to how many you can bring home.

Of course, Danny and Sheri had seen some children raised (in fact, they themselves were raised), but they were never taught to love on purpose. Instead, like most children, their observations of the world around them growing up led them to conclude that survival in life mostly comes down to attempting to successfully imitate others in your environment. So that is what they set out to do. When they became Christians, they started trying to imitate Christian behavior. But unfortunately, after a couple years, they were still pretty clueless about what a Christian parent was supposed to do.

Then one day Danny, in attempting to parent precious little Brittney, said, "Do you want me to give you something to cry about?" In that moment, his father, who left his family when he was 6 years old, popped out of his mouth, landed on the living room floor, and was going to raise Danny's daughter. It scared him! He thought, "How can someone I don't even know have such an influence on the way I see things and the way I am going to treat this child? How in the world is my father sneaking back into my life? How is my father, who only met Brittney once as an infant and has never talked to her, going to influence her life?" The answer: through Danny! A stranger was going to influence his family through the foundations that were laid very early and very long ago in his life.

WHAT WE BELIEVE

We all have a certain set of beliefs that we learned were "normal" when we were brought into this world. Our entire environment established and then reinforced those beliefs. It is human nature to surround ourselves with the teachers, coaches, employers, pastors, church leaders, and peers who will reinforce our every-day paradigms. That's why everybody close to you is largely doing what you are doing, and shares a similar faith, political affiliation, economic and social class, and value system. At some level, you're imitating them, and they are imitating you. Whenever you get around somebody who doesn't support your beliefs, that person becomes an irritant—or at least (and likely) a threat. Your response to such people, whether consciously or unconsciously, is, "You scare me! I want you way over there. I am going to gather people around me who make me feel comfortable. They help me justify how I am living." When we are successful in maintaining these comfort zones, the foundations of our society and our lives go largely unchallenged and have a lasting effect on the way we believe and behave.

The problem is that many of our versions of "normal" really don't have anything to do with Heaven's "normal." I'm not talking about what we *say* we believe to be true, but what we actually live out. As Sheri and I tried to expose and dismantle our old foundations and build new ones, we discovered that some of the foundations that many other Christians had established in their homes were not working out so well for them, either. This fueled our passion to articulate, from a scriptural point of view, what aspects of Christian parenting paradigms work or do not work and help parents see how Heaven can pass through them to their children.

Our behavior flows from our beliefs, from the way we interpret the world around us. I could give you a list of tools to use with your children, but if you use them with a paradigm that is out of line with how the Kingdom of God works, they will just cause problems. If a doctor misdiagnoses a symptom, it doesn't really matter how much the doctor knows about medicine. The prescription will be ineffective and even harmful unless the doctor accurately recognizes the problem as it really is. It is vitally important that we are able to make correct diagnoses of the problems that come before us. Our responses to circumstances will either be right or wrong, depending on the accuracy of our interpretation. If I try to change my response to circumstances, just because I know it is the right response, while continuing to perceive things the same way, I will be in conflict with myself.

Eventually, I will get worn out and go back to responding in ways that feel congruent with my perception.

Thus, this book is a *why-to* book as well as a *how-to* book. I am going to share some stories with you and give you some tools to help you accomplish real-life objectives in parenting your children. However, without establishing the fundamental core values of a godly perspective in your thinking, these skills and tools will simply be more ways to manipulate your child. That's not what I want to give to you. I want you to see the heart from which things such as freedom, respect, love, and self-control flow.

FROM THE INSIDE OUT

As I have said, when Brittney, "practice child number one," came along, Sheri and I received very few new parenting tools from our new Christian community. So, for the first couple years of her life we carried wooden spoons everywhere we went. We had wooden spoons in the diaper bag, in our pockets, in the glove box of our car, in every room in the house—even at our friends' houses. The child had nearly a cord of wood in her behind by the time she was 5 years old. Why? Because she was a "strong-willed child," and I was convinced that our job was to break that will. And when I reached into the parental toolbox as a young parent, what I pulled out was what I had been given. All I had were various sizes of hammers. I had a tool belt with nine hammers of different sizes. Imagine hiring a carpenter who showed up at your house with a truckload of hammers and said, "I am here to build your house. I brought all my hammers."

"Is that the only tool you've got?"

"Yeah, but I can build a house with just hammers. It's an ugly house. Nobody wants to live in it, but it can be done. I can measure, and I can drill a hole. I can do just about anything with a hammer."

"Hmmm, I see. No, thank you."

The hammers my father gave me were different sizes of intimidation. And behind those tools of intimidation was a set of beliefs about himself, me, and the role and responsibility of parenting that are simply incompatible with the kind of relationships that God has designed for us to have with Himself and each other. Ephesians 3:15 states that every family in earth and heaven derives its name from Father God. He designed and intended our families to express the kind of relationship that God designed us to have with Him. And if we are going to attempt to parent our children in the same way God parents us, there is a good chance that we are going to discover places in our relationship paradigm that are incongruent with how He works.

Let's review what the Bible says about how God relates to us as His children. It says that He has made a New Covenant with us (Matt 26:28). When God spoke of this New Covenant through the prophet Jeremiah, He did so in a day where the dominant cultural paradigm was that God related to humankind from the outside in (see Jer. 31:27-34). Israel had a culture of external control. If you sinned, you got leprosy. If you sinned, you got stoned—with real stones. If the nation sinned, their enemies invaded their territory. Things like the pillar of cloud guided them by day and the pillar of fire by night. They had the priests, the temple, and a bunch of other external ways to experience God. In fact, practically every aspect of daily life for God's people held some kind of external way to relate to God.

The New Covenant Jeremiah described is entirely different. He prophesied about a day when our covenant with God would move from an external experience to an internal experience. The government of Heaven would move from outside the individual to inside the individual. This was the relationship with God that Jesus would introduce through His death and resurrection. Jeremiah said:

> *"Behold, the days are coming," says the Lord, "when I will make a new covenant with the house of Israel and with the house of Judah—not according to the covenant that I made with their fathers in the day that I took them by the hand to lead them out of the land of Egypt, My covenant which they broke, though I was a husband to them," says the Lord. "But this is the covenant that I will make with the house of Israel after those days," says the Lord: "I will put My law in their minds, and write it on their hearts; and I will be their God, and they shall be My people. No more shall every man teach his neighbor, and every man his brother, saying, 'Know the Lord,' for they all shall know Me, from the least of them to the greatest of them," says the Lord. "For I will forgive their iniquity, and their sin I will remember no more"* (Jer. 31:31-34).

Now, in the external governing system, the motivating force in the relationship with God came in the form of blessings for obedience and threats of punishment—plagues, exile, and being "smitten on your hind parts" for disobedience. These revealed God's power and defined the expectations in the relationship. If the threat of punishment were to be removed, God's people would lapse into another season of rebellion against Him. This style of relationship makes it a short jump to conclude that God is in a bad mood and has issues. Unfortunately, many of us, whether believers or not, continue to raise our children according to an Old Testament paradigm. It is still common or "natural" to believe that mistakes or sin must be punished. The parenting model that flows from this paradigm presents a "punisher" role for the parent and creates an "outside-in" approach to learning about life for the child.

In the New Covenant, God relates to the believer in a new way, through writing His "law on our hearts and minds." When the law is written on our hearts and minds and when God Himself dwells in us, we no longer need to be controlled from the outside, because we have the capability and responsibility to control ourselves—to tell ourselves what to do and to make ourselves do it. The final verse in the above passage tells us why this switch in covenants could take place—"I will forgive their iniquity, and their sin I will remember no more." As long as our sin had not been punished and our hearts remained spiritually dead, we were separated from God. But on the cross, Jesus dealt with the condition that required God to relate to us from the outside. As a result, punishment, wrath, and intimidation have all disappeared from His attitude toward us. God is a *safe place*. Because sin has been dealt with in the New Covenant, we no longer need to be punished or controlled but need to learn to manage our freedom responsibly, which changes the goal of government as well as the goal of parenting. When love and freedom replace punishment and fear as the motivating forces in the relationship between parent and child, the quality of life improves dramatically for all involved. They feel safe with each other, and the anxiety that created distance in the relationships is chased away by the sense of love, honor, and value for one another.

This reminds me of a story from another family who sat through the parenting class we did at the high school. On our last week together, the mom explained that her home six weeks previously had been a place of tension. Her 15-year-old son practically lived in his room. For the previous two years, the only time he had come out was to fight with his parents about something. She then reported what had happened after they had changed their controlling parenting style to one of love and respect:

"My son came out of his room and came into the living room where his father and I were sitting. He sat down with us. I looked at my husband and raised my eyebrows and he shrugged his shoulders because neither of us knew what was going on. Our son began telling us about his day." She began to choke back tears as she continued: "He then went on to share a story with us about how much he is starting to see how disrespectful his peers are toward one another. He said that he was noticing the disrespect so clearly because the respect he feels coming from us has increased so much lately. He then asked if we wanted to play a board game." She interrupted her own story to point out what a miracle this was. "The only board game we had in the closet was…Aggravation. We could hardly contain our laughter as we headed for the table. We used to live aggravation and now we are sitting down together as a family to play Aggravation."

As believers, we will never be able to parent our children from the inside out like God does unless we fully make the switch in covenants. The problem for many of us Christian parents is that we still believe that the way God shepherds us and consequently, the way we must shepherd our children, is primarily through punishment. We think, "I didn't pray an hour this morning, so I got a flat tire on the way to work." We believe that God punishes us like this, that He is responsible to make us do the "good" things. Every time something bad happens, we trace it back to our failure, and we *know* it's part of the external government enacted by a wrathful God. We try to "make" true whatever we believe to be true, searching our experiences for evidence that supports our beliefs. But this "truth" about God simply is not true, and we need to stop drawing these sorts of connections. We need to realize that our God is a God of freedom, not a God of control. Second Corinthians 3:17 declares, "Now the Lord is the Spirit, and where the Spirit of the Lord is, there *is* liberty" (italics added). He cares about freedom so much that He was willing to sacrifice His Son to restore the freedom that we lost through sin (Gal 5:1 NASB).

The Kingdom of Heaven is not an external government. When the disciples and all the people started to realize that the King of Kings had shown up in the person of Jesus, they started asking Him, "Oh! How will you set up your Kingdom? We'll get you a big throne! Ooh, I want to be your secretary of defense! I want to be your right-hand man! I want some political favor!" They were very confused, and even a little disappointed, when they found out that Jesus didn't come to sit on a throne and establish an external government. When we train our children to obey by presenting an external threat, we handicap their understanding of how the Kingdom of Heaven works.

Now, we will not be able to introduce our children to the Kingdom of God if that Kingdom is not manifesting in our own lives. If we have not learned to live from the inside out, then it will be very unnatural for us to train our children to live that way. The reason many of us have an Old Testament parenting model is that we are still living in an Old Testament paradigm that builds an external structure to protect us from the powers of sin and death, instead of activating the power of God within us to do so. We still believe that sin is more powerful than we are. When children grow up in an environment where their parents are scared of sin, they learn to fear failure. All the methods by which they deal with their kids seem to build fear instead of love. As they work to eliminate opportunities for sin, parents develop an expectation that their children live a mistake-free life, and the goal of parenting becomes teaching obedience and compliance. As a result, their children miss the whole lesson about freedom.

CREATED FOR FREEDOM!

In the beginning, God created mankind to be free. There were no constraints in the Garden. Adam and Eve were running around naked (see Gen. 2:25)—no bras, no underwear, no bathing suits, nothing. This is God's intended version of your life: absolute freedom. But what made the Garden free? It wasn't that they were naked. No, the Garden was free because of the Tree of the Knowledge of Good and Evil. "What?" you ask. "That's the bad tree! How could that lead them to freedom?" Well, if they hadn't had the Tree of the Knowledge of Good and Evil in that Garden, they would have been trapped in a paradise prison. Without the option of making a poor choice in that environment, they would not have been free.

And so, the devil put the Tree in the Garden. No, wait. Who put the tree in the Garden? Did God, the loving Father, really put a poor choice in His beloved children's environment? "*No*, say it isn't so! God would only put them in a really safe, wonderful, perfect place like…Christian school. We must train our children in serious limitations so they will not sin." Sound familiar? (Now there are a lot of great reasons for Christian schools, but this isn't one of them.) But God was the One who did it. And where did He put the Tree? Did He say, "The naked people won't find it on Mt. Everest! It will be a long time before they get a naked expedition up there! And they can't say I didn't give them a choice. I totally did. Or we could stick it behind a thorn bush. Oh wait, there aren't any of those yet." No. He put it right in the *center* of the garden next to the Tree of Life.

This story shows us the importance of freedom to our loving Father. Without the freedom to reject Him, we are powerless to *choose* Him. Obedience is a choice. The Lord plays by His own rules. He has designed us to be free and has given us an open environment in which to exercise our freedom. But with our children, we so often opt for a different approach: "Let's see. Let's find the most perfect, trouble-free environment possible. Christian school—you guys pull all the bad trees out of the environment and I'll be back to pick you up. Don't fall away before I get back." What this reveals is that we are terrified by our children's poor choices. We try to eliminate as many as possible. The fact that we eliminate poor choices from our children's lives, while God introduced one in the garden *on purpose*, shows us that we need paradigm shift.

I want to describe a respectful interaction that I had with my two sons in which they were allowed to make some choices that ultimately taught them to exercise self-control and manage their freedom well. How many of you have children who have taken you to task over the issue of bedtime? Well, when Levi and Taylor were 6 and 4 we introduced a solution learned from *Love and Logic*® called *room time.*

Instead of ordering them to be quiet and go to bed, I told them, "It's room time. We don't want to see you or hear you until the morning."

Levi asked, "Can we play with our toys?"

"Don't want to see you. Don't want to hear you."

Taylor asked, "Can we leave the light on?"

"Don't want to see you or hear you until the morning."

"Can we read a book?"

"Don't want to see you, don't want to hear you."

"Okay!" The look on their faces said that they were thinking, "Oh my gosh, our parents are losing their minds. It's amazing!"

Now, when you put a 4- and a 6-year-old boy in a room alone together, it's like putting two puppies in a box and saying, "Don't touch each other." In moments I could hear them. So I opened the door and said, "Hey, I can hear you!"

Levi was on top of Taylor. "He jumped on me."

"Yeah, I can see that. Hey! Are you guys tired?"

"We're not tired."

"Come here and let me show you something."

They followed me out, and I took Levi into the garage. "Levi, there's the broom. When you get that all swept up, there's a garbage can. If you're tired you can go to bed, but if you're not tired I will find something else for you to do."

I took Taylor to the back patio. "Taylor, come here, buddy. When you have this back patio swept up, you can go to bed if you're tired. If you're not tired, I've got something else for you to do."

In a little while, Levi came in. "So are you tired?"

"Uh-huh."

"You want to go to bed?"

"Uh-huh."

"Alright buddy, goodnight. I love you." Off he went.

Taylor was still on the back porch, being skinned, or at least sounding like he was being skinned.

"Buddy, are you cold?"

"Yeah."

"Here's your jacket." He took forever doing this tiny chore, which was beautiful because he was experiencing his choice. In a little while, I asked, "Hey buddy, are you done?"

"Yeah."

"Are you tired, or do you need something else to do?"

"I'm tired."

"Okay, baby, I love you. Goodnight." Off he went.

The next night, I said the same thing. "Hey, it's room time. I don't want to see you or hear you until morning." Again I heard them. So I opened the door and asked, "Are you guys tired, or do you need something to do?"

In unison they said, "We're tired!"

As time moved on, I hardly ever got to do this fun stuff, because kids are geniuses. They are absolute geniuses, and if you just give them some power to practice with, if you treat them like they have a brain that works, they will make you marvel.

But one night a couple of summers ago, when Levi and Taylor were 15 and 13, I got to practice on them again. Brittney had gotten married and moved out, and for the first time in their lives they had their own rooms. It was late and I said, "Hey, it's room time. See you in the morning." They both went into Taylor's room, which I didn't notice, until I heard things crashing around back there. From the couch I yelled, "Are you guys tired?" I heard Taylor's door open and shut, and I heard Levi's door open and shut. Nine years later, it is still in the subconscious mind: "I have a choice. One of them is really dumb. I choose freedom. I choose self-control."

PEACE IN A PLAN

Do you know why God could introduce a poor choice in the Garden of Eden? He had a plan for every possible outcome, including the worst. Scripture tells us that Jesus was the "Lamb slain from the foundation of the world" (Rev. 13:8). God wasn't freaked out by the fact that we could blow it. It may seem that way when we read the Old Testament and see how He punished people for sin. But when you read the whole story, you find out that unless He showed us what sin costs us, we wouldn't have understood what the cross—His plan—would accomplish.

God can carry peace into our messes because His plan, the cross, worked. He's already dealt with the sin issue. He is going to be OK no matter what we do. The Father's attitude toward us in our sin is, "It's all right. But I need you to trust me, and I need you to hear me. We're going to be OK. We're going to make it through this. I can win with any hand that's dealt to me. You're on my side, and I'm on your side. We'll pick up that which the devil meant for evil and turn it around, and because of that I want you to come to Me in the midst of your failure. I'm not mad. I got really mad one time and I poured out all my wrath and punishment for sin on the Lamb that I supplied, because He's the only One that could handle it (1 John 2:2). Jesus was punished unto death for all your mistakes, so why would I have anger and punishment for you now? I need you to come close to me, not be afraid of me and run away. I need you to trust that I love you and that I am with you and for you. Come here."

I know that all sounds great and idealistic, but it's the truth. It's the absolute truth, and we've got to believe it or it's not going to show up in our actions. That is the heart attitude that we must communicate to our children if we are going to cultivate a right representation of the Father's love in them. Of course, in order to say this to our kids, it needs to be true in us. We need to learn how to be OK no matter what they do. When we are successful in doing that, it's not such a hurdle for them to get over their experience with us and move into the truth. When we do that, we usher them into a right relationship with an internal God who loves them, who's not freaked out about their mistakes, and who has a solution that really does work.

So, at the heart of godly parenting is the conviction that the mistakes and failures of our children are not the enemy. The real enemy is *bondage*, and if we don't teach our children how to walk in and handle freedom, they won't know what to do with it. They may stay safe through Christian elementary school and Christian college and then they will go and wrap themselves in a religious environment and say, "Control me from the outside, because if any of this went away I think I would disintegrate!" And later they will say, "I married a control freak so I wouldn't fall and we secretly and not so secretly hate each other. But we go to church." It's a big bummer. To fear our children's poor choices is to teach them to be afraid of freedom.

TRAIN UP A CHILD...

Our children are professional mistake makers. They are all on a learning journey. When we are afraid of their mistakes or their sins, our anxiety controls our responses to them and the spirit of fear becomes the "master teacher" in our home. Even though Second Timothy 1:7 clearly tells us that we've not been given a spirit of fear from God, we partner with that spirit to train our children toward the goal of obedience and compliance.

For many of us, like it was for me, intimidation is our only real parenting tool. We have various levels of intimidation. We try to convey to our kids that we are in control of their lives from the time they are tiny. Once again, the problem with that lesson is that Heaven is not trying to control your life. God doesn't want to control you. Remember, in the presence of the Lord there is freedom, not control (2 Cor. 3:17). We sing songs all day long about how God is in control. He does not control you, and neither does your wife, your boss, or your children. No one controls you. As a matter of fact, we've been given a Spirit of power, love, and self control (2 Tim. 1:7 BBE). You cannot blame your life on God.

So who is in control? You are. But if you have never learned to control yourself, then it is no wonder you are so scared. If we don't control ourselves, then we are out of control, and being out of control is a very powerless feeling. Have you ever been in the car with someone who is not driving the way you would like? You want control. You either want that steering wheel or you want out of the car. Many parents believe that when their children present failure, rebellion, disrespect, irresponsibility, or other willful or sinful actions, they must gain control by intimidating their children into changing their minds.

As Christians, we need to understand that fear is our enemy. Many of us admit this to be true but find fear much harder to get rid of. So many of us have had our paradigms shaped by a fear of punishment to the degree that we actually believe we *need* the threat of punishment to stay on course. "If I don't have a really bad consequence for making this poor choice, I'm choosing it. You can't stop me, so you better put a gun to my face." We believe that we need to be controlled from the outside. I imagine that Timothy laughed when he first read the letter in which Paul said, "You have not been given a spirit of fear, but of power and of love and of a sound mind [self-control]" (2 Tim. 1:7 BBE). In his previous letter, Paul told Timothy to drink wine for his stomach. Perhaps his stomach was upset because Timothy was a stressed-out guy. At any rate, Paul's direct exhortation that Timothy had not been given a spirit of fear implies that Timothy was afraid. He needed to leave behind the fear that he most likely learned at home. So he said, "You have not received a spirit of fear. Timothy, what God has given to you does not produce fear. God is not trying to intimidate you, and neither am I."

When I talk about training your children from the inside out, in freedom, I am talking about removing fear— specifically, the fear of punishment. Removing the training instrument of punishment is not a new concept. First John 4:18 says, "There is no fear in love. But perfect love drives out fear, because *fear has to do with punishment.* The one who fears is not made perfect in love" (NIV). It means that *all* the fear leaves your life when love comes in. There is *no* fear of punishment in love!

In order to train our children in love, our behavior as parents must reduce fear, not increase fear. What happens when you go toe-to-toe with one of your kids? What happens when one of your kids does not want to obey? What do you do when your child lies to your face? What is your response when your child gives you something ugly like disrespect? What manifests when your child resists allowing you to control him or her? As much as love casts out the fear, fear will cast out the love. Love and fear are enemies. They have completely different sources. Love is from God, and His enemy produces fear. We need some methods, tools, and skills to respond to our child's sin in such a way that we create love, not fear. But if all we have is what we were given, most of us have tools that create anxiety, because we are afraid. "I'm scared, so let me teach you a lesson. The lesson is, be afraid when I am afraid."

THERE ARE NO YELLOW TRUCKS IN HEAVEN

The idea that there is somebody who has all the control and somebody who has none is the root of all evil in relationships. That is the biggest lie you could ever teach your child. "There are two types of trucks in the world. There are red trucks and there are yellow trucks. Now, guess which one I am, and guess which

one you are. I am powerful and you are not. Lucky for you, though, I am a benevolent dictator. I am like Jesus, because Jesus is the great big yellow truck in the sky, and we are the itty-bitty, powerless red trucks, and if we are good we won't get squashed like bugs. Oh remember, He's in a good mood too—unless you tick Him off. Then you better get ready to take your medicine. I learned that in church today."

The way that we see the Father determines how we will relate to Him and how we will relate to others. Because of this, we want to be careful about how we see Him. We will teach our children what we see and teach them to relate to a God that looks like us. If I teach my children that there are red trucks and yellow trucks, guess which one they want to be? They're pretty smart. "Hey, I want to be a yellow truck. I want to be powerful in relationships. I need to figure out what to do when people don't give me my way. What am I going to do when my little brother doesn't let me control him? Or my big sister doesn't let me control her? Or my mom! My mom won't let me control her. What can I do? Dad sure seems like a big yellow truck, but someday it's going to be Dad and me in the driveway, because that's where the yellow trucks rumble, right there in the driveway."

This is a disrespect factory. You cultivate high levels of disrespect in your family system when you teach people, "There's one of us who has power, and it's not you!" Because then they go, "Oh yeah?"

And you go, "Yeah."

"Oh yeah?"

"Yeah!"

"Make me!"

"No, you make me."

"I'll make you."

"I made you first."

A back-and-forth power struggle cultivates disrespect. It is a process that assaults the peace and freedom between two people by devaluing them. It cannot help but damage the relationship.

THE MOST EXCELLENT GOAL

This false belief that you not only can, but are responsible to, control your children contributes to elevating the inferior priority of obedience and compliance in the home. The danger is that it not only leads to disrespectful interactions, but it also blinds you to what is really going on inside your child, especially if your child is compliant. It's easy to mistake obedience for a good relationship. As long as the child is doing what you say, your relationship seems fine. The moment obedience is threatened, the relationship is threatened. Therefore, in order for your children to be around you, they must become you. The problem is that if there is no real connection between your hearts and no mutual value for how your behavior affects one another, you can get compliance all day long in front of your face, but the second your children are out of your presence, they are no longer controlled by your core values. When their goal is to avoid punishment, then they have no goal of protecting your heart. When they're away from you, the punisher is gone.

We experience this dynamic when we're traveling down the highway. If a highway patrol car pulls onto the highway, everyone has to speed up! No, not usually. Most everyone is thinking, "Oh my gosh, there's a cop! I had better slow down and let him in front of me. I had better stay behind him. Oh geez. I didn't plan on there being a cop today. This is going to take forever! Who's he going to get? Shark in the water!" When the law dictates compliance, you need the presence of a punisher to protect those laws. But when my heart is connected to your heart, my decisions are designed to protect our relationship no matter how far out of my presence you are. I actually live in your presence when my heart is connected to your heart, and the deposit you have made inside my life steers me in your absence.

When the ministry of Jesus on the earth seemed to have no end in sight, He told the disciples that He had to go but that He wasn't going to leave them alone (John 16:7). He didn't say, "I want to make sure that you guys stay in line, so I'm going to leave you the Punisher. Watch your step!" Nor did He say, "I'm going to go, and to make sure you don't mess this up, I'm leaving you the Controller." No, somehow it seemed right to Him to leave us with the Helper, the Comforter, the One who comes alongside, the One who brings conviction, the Counselor, the One who reminds us. The very model that we have of Heaven's government is a Helper, a Counselor, and a Reminder—not a highway trooper. In leaving us the Comforter, He was saying, "I'm going to leave you someone who will help you maneuver your life through the abundant freedom of my Father's Kingdom."

How does the Comforter guide us into freedom? David described the way He relates to us this way: "I will instruct you and teach you in the way you should go. I will guide you with my eye upon you" (Ps. 32:8). What kind of strength does an eyeball have over a person's behavior? We all know about the "evil eye," but that's not what He was talking about. He was not saying, "Watch your step, buddy. I mean it." He was saying, "Look into my eye. What do you see? You see my heart. You see the way that you are affecting me, because it is in my countenance. I will guide you with what you see in my eyes by allowing you to see my heart and how you're affecting it. And because you value our relationship, I know you will change your decisions to protect my heart." When God leads us with His eye, we are free to choose our attitudes and behaviors based on what God shows us. He leads and we follow, or we don't.

After declaring that He was going to guide us with His eye, God compared this way of relating to one with external control. He said, "Do not be like the horse or like the mule, which have no understanding, which must be harnessed with bit and bridle, else they will not come near you" (Ps. 32:9). Dumb animals need an external control system, or else you can't get them to come around you. In essence, God told us, "Don't be like a dumb animal. Connect heart to heart, so that I can lead you with my eye. If you act like a donkey, I will have to treat you like a donkey, and if I treat you like a donkey, you will act like a donkey. If I build an external control system around you, then you will depend on it and I won't be able to remove it from you, because you won't be able to control yourself. I will have handicapped you for life, quite possibly, if I teach you that something outside of yourself is greater than that which is in you."

It doesn't matter if you're a believer and you can quote First John 4:4: "Greater is He who is in you than he who is in the world" (NASB). You don't believe it if you feel controlled by the world around you. Do you feel powerless in the face of a toddler's tantrum or a mouthy 14-year-old? If so, you're living in the old paradigm, the one that made Paul cry out, "Who will deliver me from this wretched body of death?" (Rom. 7:24).

When we practice a life of teaching our children to comply and obey through the fear of punishment, it makes it easy to misunderstand Jesus' statement, "If you love me, you will keep my commandments" (John 14:15 NASB), and think that it means that Jesus wants to control us. "Jesus wants to control me, and if I don't give Him control, He's going to *yellow truck* me somewhere. If I don't turn my tithe check in this week, He's going to break my washing machine." If you see God as the great punisher in the sky, then you think it's natural, normal, and righteous to interpret that the bad things in your life come from Him. And when you hear that God is good and He's in a good mood, you will have to reshuffle your whole paradigm or find a way to believe that it doesn't apply to you. You'll start rationalizing, "Of course He's good. Well, He's not mean. Well, He's good to the good people, but He's chasing me with a whip in the temple!"

You'll notice, by the way, that in the temple story, Jesus didn't catch anybody. Wouldn't that have been a great story? "And Jesus stood over the guy just whipping the flesh off the top of his head. Repeatedly!" You know that part isn't in there, but that's the part we like to hang on to. People who want to justify their "yellow truck" perspective say, "Well, Jesus chased them through the temple with a whip!" But poor Jesus was so lousy with a whip that He couldn't even hit or catch anybody. The better interpretation is that He wasn't trying to beat them up or punish them.

When Jesus said, "If you love me, you will obey my commandments," He wasn't saying, "Hey, we are trading the Old Testament for the *New Old Testament*. Forget the Ten Commandments and figure out what my commandments are!" He was saying, "If you love me, it will show up in the way you treat what I told you is important to me. I can see how much value you place on protecting my heart based on how you treat what is important to me."

When my oldest son, Levi, graduated from eighth grade, he approached Sheri and me with this idea. He said, "Mom, Dad, I want to go to a public high school so I can play football."

Immediately, both of us could feel adrenaline dripping into our blood streams. We thought to ourselves, "Hmm. You currently attend a small Christian school with about 12 eighth graders and about 45 junior high students in all. Now you want to go to a school that has 500 incoming freshmen and 1,800 total students. I wonder how many poor choices there are on a campus with 1,800 adolescents?"

So I said to Levi, "Son, that idea scares us pretty badly. Why would we be geniuses to say yes to this idea?"

He looked at us and saw that the door wasn't completely shut, but that it was definitely not open. He knew that we were scared, and that it was his problem to do something about the fear. He answered, "Why should you let me go to this high school? Because I will not break your heart."

Wow! If there was one answer that would have worked, he found it. He addressed the problem. We were afraid that this 14-year-old boy would not protect our hearts. We thought that this was going to become our problem to manage. But instead, he took responsibility for his half of our relationship and promised to make decisions that would value and sustain our connection.

In Matthew 7:22-23, Jesus said,

"Many will say to Me in that day, 'Lord, Lord, have we not prophesied in Your name, cast out demons in Your name, and done many wonders in Your name?' And then I will declare to them, 'I never knew you; depart from Me, you who practice lawlessness!'"

He is going to be saying that to some people who think, "I've been going to church my whole life. I've obeyed the rules. I wrote the rules on my house. I taught them to my children. We traded the Old Testament for the New Old Testament. I chased them around the house with a whip. I showed them who You are. My kids are as scared as I was. What do you mean I never knew You?" The way we live our lives shows Jesus the value we have for our connection with Him. He doesn't want to control us, but He does want our love. He is not interested in us obeying Him when there is a punisher around, only to disregard Him when we think no one is looking.

It's difficult sometimes to believe that this is true, especially as Christians, because we've been practicing the fear of punishment for such a long time. Many Christians are afraid of "being left behind" or "missing the rapture" because we know that we are not without faults. So many of us experience tremendous anxiety over whether God is pleased with us. The experience of love is not an ongoing, convincing experience for many of us. Therefore, we wrestle with the fear of rejection or punishment.

PREPARING FOR A LIFE OF FREEDOM

The heart of God toward us is that we would learn to handle tons of freedom. We've got to learn how to live in relationship with the Limitless One who does not want to control us. We've got to learn how to choose those things that build a relationship of love when we have unlimited options. Will we make choices for love, freedom, peace, honor, and truth when we could choose selfishness, pain, chaos, or lies? Are we preparing our children to constrain themselves among unlimited options or to require external constraints?

Consider one of the most famous parenting verses in the Bible. Proverbs 22:6 says, "Train up a child in the way he should go, and when he is old he will not depart from it." Clearly our job as parents is to train our children. Contrary to the way many people think, however, this verse does not say, "Train up a child in the way that you want him to go," or, "Train up a child in the way you think he should go," or, "Train up a child in the way where you always win." There is a way that your child is to go. Do you know what it is? Have you spent much time developing, cultivating, and facilitating the way that your child should go? The way our children should go is the way of freedom to be who they were destined to be.

Think of a gardener training a rose bush. He knows he needs to prune off branches and tie other ones to stakes. But he will only know which branches to prune or tie if he understands how roses grow best. God has put a design and destiny within our children. We were all designed in God's image for a relationship with Him. We are all designed and destined to co-labor with Him in that relationship to see the world around us transformed by the reality of His Kingdom. We were all designed and destined to know His love, pleasure, and goodness. And then, as we pursue our destiny to walk in relationship with Him, He unfolds the unique destiny that we each have as members of His body. He has given each of us our own story, our own chapter within the grander tale of history. As parents, our goal is really to introduce our children to relationship with God by doing our best to relate to them like God does. More specifically, God has entrusted us with the task of recognizing the unique qualities in our children that connect to His calling on their lives and helping them to develop those things on purpose. We are stewards of that way. It is part of our job to help draw this way to the surface of our children's lives. We are to help them become familiar with it so that they learn to direct themselves in that course all the days of their lives, in partnership with the Holy Spirit.

Many of us have been taught that we are to be trained up in the way that someone else thinks that we should go, and we spend the rest of our lives checking with someone to see if we are going the way we should be going. We become dependent on a voice outside of our head that makes our decisions and directs our vision. The Holy Spirit, however, operates from the inside out. We want to become apt at training our children to reach inside themselves and listen to the Holy Spirit for direction in the way they should go.

In order to do this, we need to focus on helping our kids get in touch with their hearts. When we discipline behavior rather than addressing the motives and thinking that produced that behavior in the first place, we teach them to be externally governed and prevent them from getting in touch with the source of their power to walk in relationship and direct themselves toward God's vision for their lives.

I remember hearing Bill Johnson say that he raised his kids with the understanding, "If I can deal with my child's attitude, I will have far less behavior to deal with." This is so powerful because it prioritizes the child's heart and the parent/child relationship. A big part of training our children in the way they should go is learning to stop chasing down and eliminating problem behaviors. Problem behaviors let us know that there is a deeper problem, a heart problem.

What does it take to know the heart of another person? It takes time, attention, and wisdom. We need to become students of who our kids are. It's not simply a matter of being with our kids. We don't get credit for being in the car with them as we're taking them to school. We need to have a plan and an interest in the matters of their heart and how those matters are playing out in their lives. We are students of the way they should go, and we are students in order to be master teachers instead of wardens and cops. We are shepherding their hearts and the heart of the matter, which is always *relationship*, not *behavior*.

LETTING OUR KIDS FAIL

In summary, limiting the freedom of our children in order to teach them external controls, smallness, constraints, and fear of punishment is not a strategy that works in the long run. Instead, we must teach our kids what freedom looks like, feels like, and how to prosper in it. This is the model of Heaven. That is what our Father in Heaven is doing. The best way to prepare our children to handle the multitude of options they will have as children of the King of Kings is to invest in developing a heart-to-heart connection. This connection replaces the *disrespect factory* and introduces the *honor factory*. The practice of honor will revolutionize the family system, because honor brings power to relationships and the individuals in those relationships. Honor is the antidote to the yellow truck/red truck syndrome.

One of the primary ways that we show honor to one another is by sharing power and control in our relationships. When we help our children practice using power from the time they are little, they become powerful people who are not afraid of the forces outside of them. They learn to think and solve problems. They learn to draw on the power within them, the power of the Holy Spirit, to direct their lives toward their goals in life. They become skilled at wielding decisions.

It's not wise to limit their development in these things until later in life. We wouldn't hand them a violin at 18 and say, "Hey, join an orchestra." I guess we could, but we should know that it's going to be a struggle for them. When we keep our children from experiencing what it's like to think for themselves, make their own decisions, and experience the consequences of those decisions, we either end up with compliant children who will be completely at sea when they leave the home, or rebellious children who wrestle their freedom out of our hands as soon as they figure out we've been withholding it. Many parents of teenagers look at their kids' wild behavior and conclude, "Well, they're teenagers; they just need their freedom." The problem is, they should have known their kids were born needing their freedom. They are human beings.

Therefore, we introduce freedom to our small children, and we allow them to practice messing it up while they have a safety net in our home. When we create a safe place for them to fail and learn about life, they end up saying, "This is the safest place I've got, right here at home. You can handle my mistakes. I can be myself, and you can find out about who I am. I can practice life, and I can run to you in my time of trouble, because you are an ever-present help. I want to get in your laps when I have sinned, because they are the safest place I have on this earth. There is no one who has demonstrated love like you have to me."

We want to be able to say to our children, as Jesus said to us in John 14:9, "He who has seen Me has seen the Father." He's just a super-sized version of love, freedom and a safe place. There is nothing that can separate us from His love. In order to do this, we must purpose in our hearts to maintain an attitude toward our children that communicates this message: "I will not allow anything to be more important to me than my connection to you. Your homework will never be more important to me than my connection to you. Your obedience, your respect level, and your success at chores will never be more important to me than my connection to you. There is nothing that I will allow to sever our connection on my side. And I will work to let you experience the truth of that promise so that I can help cast out the anxiety in your life."

In order to cast out anxiety in our children, we must first cast it out in ourselves. When we allow our interactions with others to increase anxiety, we invite them to show us their worst, because when people are scared, they show their worst. When they show us their worst we get more scared. So they show us more of their worst. Then we show them our worst because we're scared. When these processes of anxiety are escalating routinely, we become accustomed to blowouts and episodes of huge disrespectful interactions because we're scared. So we must commit to managing our anxiety in order to protect our connections. Loving on purpose means that we learn to let perfect love cast out all our fear, let perfect love bring out the best in us, and make perfect love the bottom line in our homes, as it is in Heaven.

POINTS TO PONDER

1. What is your bottom-line goal in raising your children? Do you see the goal of obedience and compliance directing your interactions with your children, or the goal of love and relationship directing them?

2. Why is love a greater priority than obedience?

3. Was it normal in your home growing up for your parents to use intimidation as a tool for parenting? How has this influenced your parenting style?

4. Do you recognize areas in your own life and in your parenting where you are operating in an Old Testament paradigm of external control?

5. How do parents who are not afraid of their children's mistakes respond differently to those mistakes?

6. Have you experienced the power struggles associated with the yellow truck/red truck syndrome in your home? If so, do you recognize the lie of control at work?

7. To what degree do you believe and walk in the truth that Jesus doesn't want to control you and wants to lead you through a heart-to-heart connection?

8. What is necessary for you to be able to address your children's attitudes and not merely their behavior?

Chapter 2

CHANGING OUR TRUTH FILTERS

Now, that's all pretty straightforward, right? The truth is that even if you say you believe in all that I've been saying, most of us don't believe it nearly enough to respond well to our kids in the moments of their failure. We're a lot like the two women my friend met at work one day.

My friend worked at a restaurant at Trinity Lake called the Bear Breath Café. (If you can get over the name and into the restaurant, it's actually pretty good.) One day, she waited on a couple of ladies who said, "We just got back from Vegas! We had never been there before, and we had such a great time. Do you want to hear our story?"

My friend said, "Well, it is sort of slow in here, so sure."

One of the ladies said, "OK, well, we got to this big, fancy hotel, and when we got into our room they had buckets of quarters sitting there—just for us to go down and get in the habit! We were excited, so we just headed right to the casino. We knew that we were going to win big!"

Then, before going on with the rest of the story, the lady made the following statement: "Now, I want you to know that I do not have a prejudiced bone in my body." She then went on to tell what had happened to them on their way to the casino. They left their room, headed down the hallway to the elevator, and when the doors opened, they saw three large black men standing in the elevator. The ladies got in the elevator and just stood there. Then one of the men standing behind them said, "Hit the floor." Both ladies instantly dropped face-first on the floor, WHAM! Quarters flew everywhere. The elevator doors attempted to close on the two ladies sprawled in the doorway. And the three guys behind them just busted up in hysterical laughter, which the ladies could not understand. Gasping, one of the men managed to say, "Lady, hit the floor you want to go to!" The ladies, mortified, tried to pull themselves and their quarters together, laughing nervously.

The three guys laughed the whole way to the lobby, and as soon as the doors opened, those ladies were gone!

Now, these ladies were at that hotel for a week, and when they went to check out of their hotel, the clerk gave them a bill and a card. The bill said, "Paid in full." They opened the card and it said, "Ladies, thanks for the laugh. I haven't had a laugh like that in a long time." The card was signed, "Eddie Murphy." Eddie Murphy and his bodyguards were in the elevator.

I have since heard that this was described as an "Urban Legend" on the internet, but I tell it to you as it was told to me by my friend. I've been telling this story in my workshops for fifteen years and whether it truly happened to these ladies or not, the point remains: our beliefs determine our interpretation of events. Those interpretations dictate our feelings and prepare us to then act in a way consistent with our beliefs.

These ladies didn't know who Eddie Murphy was. But this much *we* know: They *do* have a prejudiced bone in their bodies. We know that because *what you and I believe to be true is absolutely true to us*, and it determines how we interpret and respond to our environment. This process operates in every human being. Our beliefs set us up for our interpretations, and those interpretations generate feelings that we act upon. In other words, they create a reality for us to respond to. This is why several people can have the same experience or see the same event and walk away with completely different impressions of what just happened. Not only that, the human body is designed to prepare us for whatever response the situation calls for. If we are in a situation we deem to be threatening, then we experience the emotion of *fear* and our brain secretes the right amount of adrenaline so that our body is prepared to take action. We know that those ladies believed that being in an enclosed area with three black men meant *danger!* We know that because they interpreted the phrase "Hit the floor" as a threat. Adrenaline rushed through their bodies, and the behavior that followed was "fight or flight"—*boom!* As they were lying on their faces on the ground with the elevator doors whacking them on the sides, watching their quarters roll away, their brains were saying, "See! I told you! Danger!"

That is the other part of the process: *We reinforce what we believe to be true by the way we behave.* It's like a tape that just loops the same thing over and over. There are two things that this story demonstrates about that tape in our heads. The first thing it shows is that most of us aren't even aware of what it is saying. We think we believe something, but our behavior reveals that we actually believe something else. Second, that tape can be sending us messages that don't actually correspond to reality. So we can believe something is true that feels true but is really not true.

When we believe something is true and it's really not true, it creates a destructive pattern in our lives that feels normal. We laugh at these ladies because their idea of normal cost them some dignity. But for many of us, our ideas of normal are costing us much more than that. Not only do we feel that our behavior is normal, but we also feel like we are justified in our error. We end up spending a lot of energy surrounding ourselves with people who believe and behave the same way we do so we won't have to be confronted with the fact that we are living in a distorted version of reality. This makes it easier to say, "See, it's normal. Look at my family and friends." And many of us have downloaded a bunch of stuff that felt true, and still feels true, unless we confront it. This is why we must become people who are willing to examine our behavior and ask where it's coming from—people who seek the truth about reality. We certainly aren't going to be able to address the attitudes and heart behind our children's behavior if we aren't doing that to ourselves.

I hate snakes! I remember a time when even seeing one on TV would give me the chills. Watching them move across the surface of the sand was especially tough to take. I have killed a fair number of snakes simply because I believe that they are dangerous. A friend was over at our house not too long ago telling a story of being out with his family and coming across a rattlesnake that someone, like me, killed along side of the trail. My friend's son ran up to the snake and was distraught that someone could do such a thing. He cried out, "*Dad*! They killed it! Why would anyone do such a thing? Dad, why would anyone kill a snake?" I was silent during the story. His son was sitting right there while my friend went over the details of how their whole family was grieved over this incident. I was stunned. I'd never before met anyone who *loved* snakes. All my *normal* friends think like me; they hate snakes too. Now I have a friend who has *pet* snakes in his home and wants me to come and meet them. My belief about snakes is being confronted.

WHAT'S NORMAL?

As I mentioned in the last chapter, we get our idea of normal from our families, from the people who had the most direct influence over us in our formative years. Sometimes the first time we recognize this most clearly is when we leave our families to get married and start a new family. "What? You've never had ketchup on your tacos? You're kidding! I thought everyone loved tacos that way." We look at our spouse's family and realize, "Your family is weird." The funny thing is, our spouse is saying the same thing.

Part of the reason we are largely unconscious of what we really believe is that we have believed it for so long, and for the most part, we believed it long before we developed a *truth filter*—that is, the ability to separate true from false. As children, we depend on our environment to tell us what is good and what is bad. And just as we did, our children are constantly downloading information and accepting the reality that's given to them without any filter to put it all through.

We can say to our children (just as our parents probably said to us), "It's bedtime. You'd better go to bed and go right to sleep, because tonight a man with a red and white suit is going to land on our roof, slide down the chimney that we don't have, and leave presents all over the house. We are going to leave milk and cookies out." The kids go right to sleep, wake up in the morning, and go, "Whoa! There are presents! There is a bite out of the cookie! It's all true!"

"Yes, and there is also a bunny rabbit that is going to bounce around the world tonight and hide eggs all over the house. How are bunnies and eggs connected? I do not know. It's not important. He is going to leave a basket with chocolate in it. Where that comes from, I do not know either." But it's OK, because the child comes out in the morning, sees the basket of chocolate from the bunny, and concludes, "For me! I am going to eat the chocolate! It's true!"

Then we go on to explain that eating all that candy is OK because when their teeth fall out, there is a fairy that comes and swaps their teeth out for cash if they put them under their pillow.

Children don't have the ability to say, "You are full of baloney!" or, "This just feels wrong." A 5-year-old is not going to say, "Excuse me, you are deceived." In their earliest years, their whole orientation is to trust their environment and allow it to define their reality, to develop their "truth." Your *truth* is the set of beliefs about reality that you embrace as you grow up in order to interpret reality. Remember, what you believe to be true is absolutely true to you. So the question we all need to ask is, "What did I learn to be true in childhood, and are those beliefs really the truth?" This will help us to identify the truth that we are instilling in the hearts of our own children.

LIES WE BELIEVE

The lie that "we can control others" is the biggest lie in human relationships. If we can be delivered from this one, deeply rooted lie, then there is hope that we can change the dynamics that cause so much anxiety between people.

People must feel powerful in order to survive in their environment. Most of our human environments have other humans in them. For people to feel powerful around other people, they must figure out some way to get their own needs met. This dynamic leads to relational processes that introduce both true and false powers.

VIOLENCE IS POWER

Introducing violence into a relationship as a way to make me more powerful than you is as old as the cavemen. The goal of this method is both to overpower you and to intimidate you. Once I've overpowered you, you should be controlled by the threat that I am willing to continue this behavior. Remember, people must feel a sense of power in their environment. Some do this with violence, while others attempt to become powerful by giving the violent people what they want.

When an adult cannot get a child to do what he or she wants, or to stop doing something he or she doesn't want, the adult often introduces the dynamic of violence into the relationship to gain control of the child. The goal is to achieve obedience and compliance. Neither is an ignoble goal, but the method of dominance and intimidation is a direct violation of the laws of the Kingdom of God.

As parents, we must reevaluate our methods and understand the dynamics we are generating in our families. Once again, First John 4:18 teaches us, "There is no fear in love. Perfect [mature] love drives out fear, because fear has to do with punishment. The one who fears is not made perfect [mature] in love" (NIV). Our methods of discipline and training must reduce fear and anxiety and not generate them.

Right here would be a good place to address the issue of *spanking*. When I suggest that the introduction of violence into the relationship promotes a lie, I know that I am in danger of attacking a key tool for a great many parents. Hopefully, as a way to reduce your anxiety, even now, I want you to know that we have spanked each of our children at one time or another. In saying this, I want you to know that it is a very different approach than you may expect. I'll address this more later, but please know that it must reduce anxiety in our relationship when we use it as a tool.

ANGER IS POWER

The belief that violence makes me powerful is obviously destructive to relational connections and for most, is unacceptable if the relationship is to continue beyond a certain point. Nonetheless, it builds a foundation for the introduction of the next dynamic: Anger makes me powerful. If the threat of violence has been established as a way to gain power, then anger is the method of invoking this threat and accessing that power. We learn early on in relationships whose anger to fear. If we witness someone become violent toward others, then we believe that it could happen again. Submitting to the anger of these people seems like a way to avoid their violence directed toward us.

This is hard to accept for most people because we do not like to entertain the idea that we may be viewed as abusive people. We don't like the sound of being feared by those whom we love so much. But when our goal is obedience and compliance, then we must pursue a method that will produce that end. We must have control over others.

We can see this dynamic when a parent feels trapped in the car with his or her child, who is misbehaving. "If I have to pull this car over and come back there, you are going to be sorry. Knock it off right now, or I am going to pull this car over. I mean it!" All this is to convey a sense of power. What are we going to do if we pull the car over? We will introduce violence. But for now, we are hoping that our angry threats will bring about the same result.

WE CAN BE CONTROLLED AND CONTROL OTHERS

Consistently experiencing someone's punishing anger and demand for control leads us to believe that we can be controlled. The practice of yielding our self-control to avoid punishment builds into our beliefs the conviction that this is happening without our cooperation, that we have no other option than to give the angry person what he or she wants from us. We learn powerlessness in the presence of our parents and thus are the victims of their anger. Hence, we come to believe that we can be controlled by others and are introduced to a devastating dynamic: blame.

Blame is simply giving away the power to direct and change my life to someone else. When I blame someone, I have said, "I cannot change unless you change. I cannot forgive unless you change. I cannot love unless you change. I cannot be free unless you let me out of prison." The habit of blame comes from believing that we are powerless in our relationships. It feels real to tell ourselves that we are not responsible for how we are behaving. We are not responsible because something or someone more powerful in my external world is more powerful than I am inside.

Unwilling to live without power, people afraid of being controlled by others seek a way to control others. If I can be controlled, then other people can be controlled, and therefore I can control others. We hear phrases as children such as, "You make me so angry!" "If you hadn't said that, then I wouldn't have had to slap you." These and other experiences build into us the false belief that we can make other people behave certain ways. Violence, anger, and threatening to introduce these into the relationship become the common practice between people trying to feel powerful.

Violence = Power

Anger = Power

"Others can control me."

"I can control others."

We learn some things at home that are really not true, but boy, do they feel true, because we are still enforcing them by what we do. How do you respond now when someone is angry? How do you respond now when someone doesn't do what you want him or her to do? You reach into your belief system and you say, "You know what? I can make things happen. Watch this." And people will run around, especially if we introduce some anger and they are little people. That reinforces those lies, because you used your magic powers, and things happened. This is why we want to be careful and review what we believe to be true.

Nobody Controls You but You

So how do we create a new normal in our homes? We begin by getting a revelation of an important truth.

Author Steven Covey tells of riding in a subway car, exhausted from a long day of work, and enjoying his peaceful ride home. The subway stopped, the door opened, and in walked a man and his four children. The children began to amuse themselves by running back and forth from one end of the car to the other, screaming all the way. Covey, who was trying to enjoy his trip home, grew increasingly frustrated by how this father simply allowed his offspring to run rampant through the compartment, seemingly oblivious to their behavior. Eventually, one of the children stumbled over an elderly lady sitting on her bench. She yelped, and the guy had finally had enough. He jumped up, walked over to the father, and said, "Hey! Don't you see what is going on with your children in this car?"

The man looked up at him in a sort of daze, and in a detached voice he replied, "Oh, I am sorry. We're returning from the hospital. Their mother just died. I am sure they don't know what to do."

Stunned by this information, the upset man said, "Oh. I am so sorry. Stay right there. Let me help you with your children."

The agitated man went from angry to helpful in an instant. Why? Because he just got some new information. He received a revelation. What he believed to be true about the situation changed in an instant. And the behaviors that flowed from those respective belief systems changed right along with it.

The following statement is the revelation that we need to get if we are going to align our relational paradigms with the truth: *You can't control other people, and nobody can control you but you.* Someone can stick a gun in your mouth and say, "Deny Jesus Christ." And you still have two choices.

Realizing this truth is the key to taking the initiative to control yourself and stay true to your convictions. The ability to manage your children and yourself toward the goals that you have in being a parent rests in the ability to *tell yourself what to do and do it* no matter what they've done or are doing. Can you manage *you* no matter what your kids are doing? Just as God is able to say to us, we want to be able to say to our kids, "I will be a loving, respectful parent no matter what you do."

But so often, we give our self-control away to the mistake of our child—or our spouse, our parents, our friends, or others. When we give our self-control away, our thinking turns off and our emotions kick up. And when our emotions get flailing around, it's a little like being intoxicated—filled with poison.

When our brains don't work so well and we've got dangerous emotions bouncing around like fear and anger, watch out. This is where we get into trouble.

Angry, fearful reactions to people's mistakes reveal that somewhere in our minds still lurks that fundamental belief of the Old Covenant, not only that people *can* be controlled but that they *need* to be controlled, and they need to be controlled through punishment. They need to experience the pain of our anger so that they won't make mistakes that cause us to feel out of control. We think: "I must control them so I can have some control over the quality of my own life."

FEAR OR LOVE

When we allow the mistakes of others to manage us, to dislodge us from our goal of being loving and respectful, what we are actually submitting to is a spirit of fear. Fear is the primary thing that reigns in the life of a victim, in the life of a person who is motivated by an external system of controls. Remember, "…fear has to do with punishment" (1 John 4:18 NIV). Fear and intimidation cannot help but rule the household of those who believe they can and must control each other when they make mistakes, and use anger and violence to do it.

What's even more destructive is that such fear-driven beliefs and behavior are often identified with love. When my wife was a teenager, she got into verbal spat with her father. During the exchange he slapped her across the face. Shocked, she stood there holding her cheek that was on fire. He moved toward her, grabbed her by the shoulders, and yelled in her face, "Tell me you love me!" Love was a hundred miles away at that moment. She simply hardened her heart toward him and rode out some difficult years ahead. Most all of us as parents have things we've done to control our children that we are not proud of, but we try too often to turn these debacles into messages of love. Once again, fear and love are totally at odds with each other: "There is no fear in love. But perfect love drives out fear because fear has to do with punishment. The one who fears is not made perfect in love." If we want to create a *normal* for our family relationships in which love rules our interactions, then we simply must refuse to partner with any and all fear and punishment.

The Holy Spirit who lives within us equips us with all we need to respond to our kids and everyone else in our lives without fear—in fact, to respond to them in a way that drives out fear. It's important that we understand that the Holy Spirit is the true Spirit of *power*. Anger and violence are false powers that we grab onto when we are controlled by fear. The reason we have been given the Spirit of power is that we need power. It takes power to hold onto your self-control and manage yourself in the presence of temper tantrums, disrespect, and other childhood crises. In the face of these things, it's a really good day when you can control yourself all day, and on that really good day you should hear, "You told yourself what to do, and you obeyed you! Congratulations! Now take a nap. You are probably exhausted." The reality is that walking in the spiritual fruit of self-control is *supernatural*. But as believers who have been raised from the dead and have the Spirit of God living within us, supernatural is exactly what our lives should be.

The fruit of the presence of God in our lives is self-control:

"But the fruit of the Spirit is love, joy, peace, patience, kindness, goodness, faithfulness, gentleness, self-control. Against such things there is no law" (Gal. 5:22-23 NIV).

Now, the cool thing is that when we believe that we are the only ones who can control us and we exercise that power of self-control toward loving God, our spouses, and our children, we are partnering with the Holy Spirit and inviting His kingdom to reign in our homes. But when we partner with a spirit of fear, we invite the kingdom of intimidation, manipulation, and anger to reign. The spiritual environment in our homes really boils down to the presence of either fear or love. No matter what your intentions or goals are as a parent, the fact is that you are cultivating a loving or fearful spiritual environment in your home, and that is what is really influencing your children.

THE POWER OF OUR WORDS

The ruling spirit of our environment is made manifest through the words we choose. It is vital to realize the power that is released when you push wind over your vocal cords. The Greek and Hebrew words for *spirit* are also the words for *breath* and *wind*. What is it that passes over your vocal cords when you speak? It is spirit. This is why the Bible says, "Life and death are in the power of the tongue" (Prov. 18:21) and, "Out of the heart,"—or *spirit*—"the mouth speaks" (Matt. 12:34). As you speak, you create spirit in your environment.

Words are a spiritual catalyst. Any of us raised in a hostile environment, where a spirit of fear was the dominant principality, know that the words in the environment were perpetuating that fear. Those raised in a peaceful environment know that words, and the way people spoke them to one another, cultivated, preserved, and protected that peace. We are creating an atmosphere with the very words that we choose to use. Understanding that bumps my "mouth permit" to a new level of responsibility. Mama's old admonition, "If you can't say anything nice, don't say anything at all," is now, "Don't empower evil spirits in your environment." And if you don't have something good in your heart, work on your heart. Don't let it out of the cage. Don't just get in the habit of saying, "I'm sorry. I didn't mean to say that. I'm sorry. I shouldn't have said that. Will you forgive Mommy and Daddy for the way that we have trained you and the atmosphere that we've created around you?" Once again, if we are going to try to help our children steward their own hearts and take responsibility for the source of their words and behavior, then we simply must be already doing that ourselves. Our children are not going to lead in creating the atmosphere in our homes. They may try. They may have sunny personalities. But if you don't change, you will be the cloud cover.

Of course, our actions flow out of our hearts as well, and thus contribute equally to the spiritual atmosphere. They can even speak louder than our words, especially when it comes to setting boundaries with our kids, which we'll discuss in a later chapter. But we can't forget that when we open our mouths, we're dealing with life and death. Our job is to create a steady stream of life-giving words into our children's lives. When we learn to look at our children and see their potential and destinies in God, and learn to release the power of life through our words, we become a channel for God to broadcast His heart and His grace into them. Our words have the ability to create things in the hearts of our children. They also reach in and pull things that have always been there to the surface.

One day years ago, my wife, Sheri, got a call from the school asking her to come and pick up our son, Levi. Levi had been having a tough time. He was in second grade and wasn't reading, and the unfortunate thing about school is that they want you to read and write. To him, going to school meant having an incredibly painful experience day in and day out. Well, this was another day at school, so Sheri went to the school to pick him up. When she got there, he was waiting in front of the school with his backpack.

Sheri thought to herself, *Here we go. My words are spirit and I carry vision for my son. I carry it in my heart and in my life. I carry what it is that I want him to have.*

"Hey, rough day?" Sheri asked him.

"Stupid backpack!" He got in the car.

Sheri drove to the store and went inside with Levi. He just trailed behind. Then she stopped halfway down the aisle, turned to him, and said, "Levi, my son, who I am so proud of." With one eye, he barely looked at her.

In the next aisle she stopped and pointed at him. "Levi, my son, who I am so proud of." Still he avoided her face.

A couple of aisles later she said it again. "Levi, my son, who I am so proud of." Again, there was little response.

They got back to the car and headed to the post office. In the car she reached over to Levi, put her hand on his chest and said, "Levi, my son, who I am so proud of." This time he looked at her with a bit of belief in his eye.

They got home and started unloading the groceries. When Levi walked in with a bag of groceries, Sheri pointed at him and said, "Levi, my son…"

And this time he interrupted her with a smile and finished her sentence. "Who you are so proud of."

To this day, Sheri or I can say, "Levi, my son…" And Levi will say, " I know, I know. Who you are so proud of."

It is crucial that when your children look into your eyes, regardless of the circumstances bearing down on them, what they see is someone that believes in them. You have the power to call "those things which do not exist as though they did" (Rom. 4:17). But that same power causes devastation when a child encounters an angry, irresponsibly mouthed parent. That is death to the heart and vision of a child. As parents, we especially carry this powerful responsibility. We are very powerful. Point that power carefully.

POINTS TO PONDER

1. Have you ever discovered that what you thought you believed to be true wasn't consistent with how you actually responded to a situation, particularly when you experienced a strong emotion, such as fear or anger? Describe the situation and what you learned about your beliefs.

2. Why is blame so destructive?

3. Why is it important to be able to tell yourself what to do and to do it? Where do you need more of the fruit of self-control in your life?

4. People can exercise a lot of wit and discipline in order to stay in line and avoid punishment. How is this different from the supernatural fruit of self-control?

5. Why is it more important and more powerful to be motivated by the goal of being a loving and respectful person than the goal of never making any mistakes?

6. Do you allow the mistakes of other people to get you off track in your goals of being loving and respectful? If so, do you recognize the spirit of fear at work? Do you believe that God has the power you need to stay true to your priorities?

7. What is the spiritual environment you are creating with your words? Do you practice speaking life and destiny into the lives of your children?

Chapter 3

PROTECTING YOUR GARDEN

Let's examine some of the practices that these changes in our beliefs require. I've mentioned several times that we need new methods that build love instead of fear. In these next three chapters, I want to present you with three different responsibilities that you must embrace as a parent in order to establish a punishment-free, love-filled, respectful environment in your homes. These three responsibilities all flow directly from the core values and truths we've been discussing. To summarize, our goal as parents is to teach our children to walk in healthy relationships. The heart of healthy relationships is love, and by its nature, love requires a choice. Thus, the fundamental thing we want to give to our children is the ability to exercise and govern their power of choice so they can direct it toward love. In reaching this goal, your first responsibility as a parent is to take care of and manage yourself, which we will consider in this chapter. Your second responsibility, which we'll consider in the next chapter, is to set and enforce healthy limits with your children by giving them choices and consequences. And in the final chapter, we'll consider the third responsibility, which is to lead your children to have a high value for their connection with you by helping them understand how their choices affect your relationship, particularly when it comes to helping them clean up their messes.

BEING A GATEKEEPER

Second Chronicles 23 tells the story of a revival that took place in Israel when Joash became king. Since Joash was only 7 years old when he was crowned, the prime mover in this revival was actually the priest, Jehoiada. One of the significant things that Jehoiada did is recorded in verse 19: "And he set the gatekeepers at the gates of the house of the Lord, so that no one *who was* in any way unclean should enter." Apparently, a huge part of getting Israel's relationship with God back on track and restoring the temple of God was making sure that the temple was protected from intruders.

I believe that the same idea holds for us as parents. We are the temple of the Holy Spirit. And as parents, we are gatekeepers, not only of our own lives, but also of our families. The health and happiness of our families is directly related to our health and happiness as parents. We are creating the atmosphere. We are imparting to our children who we are. And unless we learn to sustain and protect our individual health and happiness, it won't be too long before we are imparting unhealthiness and unhappiness to our children. We can only offer to others what we ourselves have.

Taking good care of our children begins with learning to take care of ourselves. This is what we learn every time we get on an airplane. When flight attendants go through their spiel, they are explaining what to do if there's a drop in cabin pressure: Put your oxygen mask on first and then help your kids and neighbors get theirs on. If you don't take care of yourself, you won't last long trying to take care of another person. You have to have a high value for taking good care of *you!* Somewhere along the road, somebody taught us that a worn-out, burnt-out, frustrated, bitter parent is a good one. Somehow that's holy and noble. Actually, it's a sign that you're not getting enough oxygen.

In order to take care of ourselves, we need to learn how to set up healthy boundaries with our children. We need to put a *fence* around our yard, complete with a *gate*.

When our family moved back to Weaverville years ago, we discovered that there were two types of gardeners. There were those who had been doing it for a while, and those who had just moved up from the city and were going to start fresh. Now, all the people who had been doing it for a while had this big wire contraption in their yard. It was hideous, usually with old dead vegetation hanging on it everywhere. When you pulled into the neighborhood you'd see it and say, "What an eyesore that is! Why would anybody have one of those in their yard?" The new people would say they were not going to have one of those things. "We're not going to do that; that's disgusting!"

We watched as spring rolled around and all the gardeners went outside to till their soil, put the seed and the irrigation systems in, and get everything all nice. Day after day they would come out and take care of their gardens, and day after day would find encouraging evidence that it was working. Little green leafy things started popping out of the dirt. Day after day, they took care of that green leafy material. You could feel the excitement growing as the day approached when they would harvest the fruits of their labors. Then one day, the new, inexperienced gardeners came out to their gardens and found something different. Their beautiful green leafage had been reduced to sticks popping out of the ground! A wave of shock and disbelief hit them, and then rage began to rise up. They were angry, devastated, and offended. *"How could this have happened?"* It's called nature. Nature happened. They were the victims of Trinity County's deer population.

Now, across the street were the experienced gardeners, who had deer lying peacefully on the lawns outside their gardens. Day after day, these gardeners would bring out whatever they chose to give to the deer. These gardeners were not afraid of the deer. They didn't hate the deer. They didn't want to kill the deer. In fact, they loved the deer. The deer kind of added to the aesthetics and ambience of their idyllic, gardening lives.

Parenting is a lot like gardening in Weaverville. As a parent, you must find a way to set a fence around your garden with a gate. Then you must choose who comes in and who goes out, so that you can protect the quality of your life. You are solely responsible for the quality of your life. It is not somebody else's fault. It is not the deer's responsibility to take care of your garden! Just because you think you are being nice and sacrificial and long-suffering and patient and kind doesn't make you any less devastated when you discover that your children, or maybe your spouse or your in-laws, are not herbivores or carnivores but *opportunivores*. And they are looking for a chance to feast off the richness of what you have in your life. You have to be aware of this situation. You have to have a value for what you have inside you, and take personal responsibility for the garden that is yours to tend. It's not somebody else's responsibility.

Boundaries communicate value for what is inside of those boundaries. If you have several junk cars out in a field, it's called an *eyesore*. If you put a fence around those cars, then you have a *wrecking yard*. And, if you put a building around those cars you have a *garage*. With each increase of limits, you increase the value of what is inside. When you raise the level of what you require before you will allow access, you increase the value of what you have. To all who are near, we send a clear message about the level of value we have for ourselves by the way we establish boundaries.

Now, I tell the deer story because some Christian parents tend to be more passive and nonconfrontational with their children. Passive parents have no fence around their gardens because the passive relational style says, "Your needs matter; mine don't." Often, these parents struggle to get a respectful response from their children because they've done a good job communicating to their kids that they do not respect themselves. Their own needs are not important to them, so why would the children value what their parents need in the relationship?

There are also Christian parents who are more aggressive and teach their kids that it's the children's job to keep a safe distance from them. They have an electric fence around their garden. Get too close and you'll get zapped. Their aggressive style says, "My needs matter; yours don't." There are some serious yellow truck/red truck lessons going on in these homes.

But neither of these styles is what we want to teach our children because in both cases, someone is being disrespectful. We want them to learn that in a healthy, respectful relationship, the needs of both of us matter.

Another key to setting healthy boundaries is telling those around you what you will be doing instead of trying to get others to do something for you. This key is also used in the *Love and Logic*® program. As parents, it is easy to get into the routine of barking out commands. "Pick that up! Come here. Stop being so noisy. Be nice to your brother!" Our homes are filled with the illusionary practice of controlling each other. But since we no longer believe that hocus pocus, what then shall we do? Begin telling others what you will do instead. Practice being powerful by controlling something you *do* control, namely, yourself. Say things like, "I will listen to you when your voice is as soft as mine. Take your time." Or, "I will manage your fight with your brother, just like a referee. Only I charge ten dollars each for each fight I referee. Ready? Go!" When we make these statements, we have the ability to enforce what we say is important to us, and it doesn't require other people to give us control over them. We simply control what we can control.

I heard of a lady who did a great job of making sure that she told her son what she was going to do instead of trying to make him do something he didn't want to do. One day she came home from work and encountered her 9-year-old son in his soccer uniform. He said, "We've got to go to the game, mom! You said we would go as soon as you got home."

She said, "OK. Did you get the vacuuming done?"

He said, "Mom! I didn't have time. I have only been home for two hours!"

She said, "Probably so. I will be glad to take you to your soccer game as soon as the vacuuming is done. Take your time."

He said, "What! You're not going to take me right now?"

She said, "I will be glad to take you as soon as the vacuuming is done. Take your time."

"*Uh*! That's not fair!"

"I know."

"You said that if I signed up for soccer that I had to be on time, and that I was supposed to be responsible."

"That's true. And as soon as the vacuuming is done, I will be glad to take you."

"The coach is going to be really mad at you! I'm the goalie!"

"That could be. I'll be glad to take you to your soccer game as soon as the vacuuming is done."

"Vacuuming is women's work!"

"Nice try." Then she left the room, because she wanted to get as far away from his mouth as she could get. And in a few minutes she heard a noise. It was the vacuum cleaner. Shortly thereafter, her son came to her and said, "OK, I'm done. Can we go?"

She said, "Well, of course we can." She checked the floors out and said, "They look great. Let's go."

FUN, OR NOT FUN? THAT IS THE QUESTION

Learning to set respectful boundaries is an art that requires great wisdom and consistent practice. First, you will need wisdom to understand yourself. By this I mean you will need some feedback from your environment. The people closest to you can let you know how you affect the relationships around you or how you seem to be affected by the people around you. If you are passive and afraid of confrontation, you may or may not realize how it determines your relational style. The people who observe this firsthand in your life are some of your greatest sources of input. If you are aggressive and not fun to be around, then it is necessary to recruit some courageous people to confront you. Making these kinds of changes can be difficult, but they will strengthen your ability to create an improved quality of life for you and those you love.

As important as it is to understand yourself, it is equally important to understand what sort of "garden invader" you are dealing with. Your discovery will lead you to determine the kind of limits you need to set. For some of us, our greatest invader is like a little cotton-tailed bunny rabbit that comes and nibbles. In those cases we need a two-foot chicken wire fence. At other times we have deer trying to get into our garden, so we need an eight-foot hog-wire fence, maybe with a top on it. And some of us live with Brahma bulls and need razor wire and electricity. These various types are known by the way they respond to lower levels of limits we set. If we set a limit with someone in our life and he or she seems to disregard it, then we begin intensifying the boundary to help that person realize how important this area is to us. But know your predator, because if you use chicken wire on a Brahma bull, it won't even notice, and if you use electricity on bunny rabbits, you are prepping for dinner. You will need to practice with these limits as well as be aware of how your limits are affecting other people in your relationships.

One of the limits I set with my kids when they were toddlers, which I learned from *Love and Logic®*, was called *fun to be with*. It means: "This is what it takes to be around me for very long." Have you ever seen a 2-year-old who isn't fun to be with? We use the *fun to be with* tool to convey to our children, "I hope you can respect what I need in order to be around you. As soon as you start having fits, that is no fun."

You want your child to learn early on that there are two people in this relationship. That means that there are two sets of needs. You are going to supply your child's need for safety, freedom, honor, and power. You also need to teach this child that you need the same things. Most of us can't, and shouldn't, put up with "not fun" for very long. If we stay in that condition for too long, guess what is going to happen to us? We are going to become "not fun to be with" ourselves. When we are not fun to be with, and they are not fun to be with, guess what suffers most? Our relationship.

Imagine a toddler who is doing what I call the Pterodactyl call. *Yeeaak! Yeeaak! Yeeaak!* You know the one I am referring to? For me, this is definitely not fun to be around. So, quite quickly and efficiently, begin this process:

"Whoa! Hey, no fun. Fun or room?"

"*Yeeaak!*"

"You decide or I decide."

"*Yeeaak!*"

"Walk or get carried?"

"Yeeaak!"

"No problem."

"Yeeaak!"

You carry the child to the room. Upon reaching the room, you inform him or her, "You can come out of the room when you are fun. Take your time." Then you leave the room. Now, guess where that little one is? You guessed it, right on your heels. You spin around and say, "Fun or room?"

"Yeeaak!"

"No problem," you say, and start heading for the child. "Walk or be carried?"

The toddler, who was born to be free, takes off running to his room because he refuses to be hauled there one more time.

In an internal dialogue, the toddler is saying to himself, "That's right! You did not put me in my room! I put myself in this room. That's right! Mess with me! Ha! Wait a second. What am I doing in this room? Am I in a time-out? I'm two. Am I supposed to be in here for two minutes? What's a minute, anyway? I am not staying in here. No one can make me. I am coming out." And the toddler leaves the room and begins cautiously reentering the adult's space.

Meanwhile, you are in the kitchen doing dishes. Looking out of the eyeball in your ear, you say with a big smile, "Hey you! Fun or room?"

This toddler is confused by the smile. He was searching for the angry adult. You look happy. How can this be?

He may play the *no fun* card again, but eventually he will realize, "Wait. Are you kidding me? You mean you're just trying to get me to smile at you? Well, I tried *room* twice. So, here goes..." And that toddler will give you a smile.

"There's a smile! There you go! That is *fun to be with!*"

And there concludes the lesson in self-control. Your child soon learns that there are two sets of needs in any relationship. Meeting both sets are important, no matter how old or young you are. If we are to practice love and honor, then even our toddlers must practice. It is very important that we teach our children that we require respect and self-control in order to share an environment with them. It is amazing how quickly they pick it up and how smart they really are.

My son, Taylor, is our youngest. He has been parented this way since birth. Once when he was about 2 years old, he was trying to pull his sippy cup through the bottom of the top rack of the dishwasher. He began throwing a fit. I said, "Hey, hey! No fun! Fun or room?" He smiled at me and said, "Fun!" In about one second he chose fun. You see, children are amazing. They possess self-control and powers to think and problem solve that we all too often do not expect them to exercise, and so they don't. Give them a chance and I'm sure they will impress you.

Now, when we set respectful boundaries with our kids, we train them to set their own boundaries. One of the greatest joys that I have had is getting to see my children set limits in their relationships with other people. They have learned to require respect in relationships, even from adults.

I believe that setting respectful boundaries with them has also helped them to understand more about how the Lord interacts with them. Have you ever noticed how the Holy Spirit is attracted to some things and is repelled by other things? Have you ever noticed that when we are fun to be with, the Holy Spirit is there? But when we get all bitter and punishing in our attitude, we end up asking, "Where did the Holy Spirit go?" We do not feel His peace or His presence. He says, "Wow! How is this going to work out for you? Do you remember what is important to Jesus? Do you remember what He said to do in moments like this? Do you want my help with this one or do you want to figure it out yourself?" (John 14:26). Finally, when we repent, what do you know? We experience His presence again. "Fun to be with" is a lifelong key to relationship.

DISCONNECT THE BIG RED BUTTON!

Now, as our kids get a little older and a little smarter, their "not fun to be with" episodes are going to become more sophisticated. In short, they're going to learn to talk back to you, and when they're not being fun, that talk can look like defiance, arguments, and disrespect. And that's the big red button on the chest of most Christian parents—*disrespect*. Parents do all they can to keep the children from ever pushing this button. They know how crazy this makes them feel inside, so it becomes a priority to teach that no one is disrespectful to the parents, ever!

A kid starts thinking, *I am feeling kind of powerless today. I want to feel powerful.* Sure enough, the kid spits out something disrespectful and the parent goes, *"Waaaa!"* It's not that tough for a child to send his or her parent right over the edge of self-control. Simply firing a disrespect missile will usually do the trick. Children, quite naturally, find out that parents are defenseless against disrespect. Thus, parents are terrified by it.

It's a major bummer for us when we let our children control us with this fear, because their respect level goes down. It goes down because it's very scary for them to turn their lives over to a person that they can control. It's very difficult to trust a leader that you control. So we need a way to manage ourselves so these guys will have no success in pushing our buttons, no matter which way they poke and prod our psyche.

Your children are learning right in front of you, and you must understand that you cannot take their learning personally. The fact is that the problems your kids are dealing with are the same problems that every other kid on the planet is dealing with. Everywhere I go, I poll parents on the kinds of issues they're facing with their children, and without fail, the list is pretty much the same everywhere—disrespect, disobedience, irresponsibility, tantrums, whining, sibling rivalry, back-talking, bullying, low self-esteem, chores, or homework. These problems that we have with these little people are pretty universal human problems. They're happening all over the planet. They're happening in China right now. This very second, somebody is backtalking his parent somewhere in the world. These issues are not a reflection of what you did to your children. *It's not your fault*. These children are on a learning journey. Let them learn.

Parents who think that their child's problem is their problem end up in trouble. In fact, they end up feeling just like the person they're trying to fix—miserable. When they take their child's mistakes personally, they are effectively allowing their child's shortcomings to determine who they are. The only way we can *respond*, rather than *react*, to our kids' mistakes is to stay disconnected from those mistakes.

I received an email recently from a young mom who had a breakthrough in this very area:

Danny,

Hello! I just had to share a great story with you.

On Saturday night I watched a video from your *Loving Our Kids on Purpose* DVD set. Something huge stuck out to me. You talk about setting limits with our kids in such a way that we're not supposed to react to them manifesting—shouting, screaming, whatever—because it takes away from the lesson they're about to learn. That was a milestone for me! More than just a light bulb came on; floodlights came on!

So, the next day my 4-year-old daughter wanted to do something. I said that she certainly could as soon as three things were cleaned up first. I showed her the three little projects she had to complete and then went back to what I was doing. My husband was sitting on the couch while this was going on. Sure enough, she threw herself on the floor and began full-on manifesting. It was pretty. :) She protested and all that. She even changed the subject and told me how awful I was. She screamed harder and louder than she's ever screamed. It took all the self-control we had to *not* do or say anything other than "I know." But we did it. And I kept my voice calm and sincerely sad for her the whole time while I kept doing my own cleaning up. My "I know" was never a bark! That was huge! This went on for maybe 20 minutes. She actually got herself so worked up that she asked me to hold her. Now, in the past I would have put her responsibility on pause to comfort her. This time, though, I said, "I would be glad to hold you as soon as those three things are done." She screamed more than ever before…let me tell you! And I kept saying, "I know." Then, Danny, I watched her through the corner of my eye pick up and do *every* thing I asked her to do and in the order I demonstrated. There was no forgetting on her part. She knew what she had to do, and once she decided to do it, it was done perfectly. I smiled the biggest smile ever and under my breath shouted, *"Yes!"* It was beautiful. It worked, Danny! Afterward, she said, "Now, mama, would you hold me? "And I said, "Sure. I'd love to hold you." That was that.

It was the best day of parenting ever because of that half hour.

Thanks, Leslie

After reading this story, you all might be thinking, "Well, what about that child's disrespect toward her mother?" That's the big red button, remember? The kid couldn't figure it out when she tried over and over to push her button and nothing happened. At that point, the child realized that mom was a very powerful person. But the thing to see is that this mom had no button. "I'll be glad to hold you as soon as you are done." She did not tell her daughter what she had to do. She did not threaten her life. She didn't show her one of the "hammers." She told her what *she* was going to do, and then she did it. She is a very powerful woman, not controlled by another human being. And this little girl learned that she was the sole owner of her problem and should find a solution for it quickly.

MENTAL PAUSES

You may have noticed that besides telling her daughter what she was going to do, this mother had some very simple, very *short* responses to her protests. She kept saying, "I know" while her daughter threw a fit. "I know" "Probably so," "That could be," "I don't know," and "Nice try" are some of my favorites. These one-liner phrases from *Love and Logic®* are your best friend when your child wants to argue with you. They are your sanity. They are a way for you to kick your brain into neutral while the other person is trying to drive you into the Crazy Ditch. They help you to become sort of like a cloud, something that doesn't react—something that cannot be controlled. I'm not talking about stonewalling or ignoring your child. Remember, you want to create an opportunity for your child to find a solution because he or she really does have a problem. You can really only use these successfully when your attitude toward your child is one of love and trust. Love for them makes you jealous for them to learn how to do this.

When your kid is throwing a fit, giving birth to a cow right there in front of you, it is absolutely the worst time to have a reasonable conversation with that person. Your child is absolutely emotionally wasted. This would be a good time for you just to be a cloud. "I know. Probably so." And the kid will finally say,

"You're no fun to be around. I am out of here." This is what you're hoping for anyway. Off he goes to figure it out. Maybe later, when the thinker comes back, you might be able to work through the issue, but when your child is out of control, it is the worst time to engage in the struggles. Your child is not looking for solutions; he or she is looking for victims.

That can be you if you so desire, but remember—you have a choice. If you're not up for being a victim, then I encourage you to get the following one-liners down cold. Get them tattooed on your arm, inside your hand, or on the inside of your eyelid. You need some way to have these on hand so when your kid says, "That sucks! That's stupid! That's not fair!" the automatic pilot turns on.

This is what a possible dialogue with these one-liners would sound like:

"This is stupid! It's not fair!"

"I know."

"You know it's not fair?"

"Probably so."

"This is the meanest thing you have ever made me do!"

"That could be."

"Why are you acting like a freak?"

"I don't know."

You are telling your child, "I am the cloud and cannot be moved. Yes, I love you, and I am OK while you struggle with your problem and figure out where you put your respect, I am the cloud. I am going to manage me while you struggle with you. I do not control your attitude or your mouth. The moment I try, I will begin to lose this battle."

When you sow seed, you grow that sort of plant. When you try to control another human being, you are sowing seeds of disrespect. I don't care if you think you are the parent and the king of the planet, it doesn't matter. You don't get to control another human being. There are no yellow trucks in Heaven! When you try, you are being very disrespectful. But don't you worry, because harvest time is coming. And it comes about the time they are not afraid you are going to kill them anymore—adolescence. They are a little more powerful, and they start to say things like, "That's not right! That's not fair! You can't control me! I am going to do it anyway, and there is nothing you can do stop me." If we continue to try to control people who are starting to feel powerful, watch out. Those kinds of power struggles will seriously damage your relationship with your children.

"OH NO" AND "NO PROBLEM"

"Oh no" and "No problem" are also responses particularly designed to help your children take ownership of their mistakes and problems. When your child makes a big, fat, hairy mistake, you need to be able to respond, "Oh no." And make sure they can feel the love in this, because "Oh no" means, "I am so sad for you, and I know this is going to hurt some. But it is going to be OK, because I know that you are as smart as anybody else, and you are going to learn something from this consequence that is coming down the pike. Do you hear that? It's not a freight train; it's a consequence, and it's coming to a set of tracks near you. I love you very much while this is going on in your life."

I want my children to feel the weight and responsibility of their decisions. I want them to practice and learn about life in a way that resembles the real life that will come their way in adulthood. For example, imagine your daughter coming home from school and announcing this:

"Uh, mom, I left my backpack on the bus."

"Oh no! You left your backpack on the bus."

"Uh huh."

"Oh no."

"Uh, yeah. Uh, mom, uh, well, uh, I took Spooky, my hamster, to school today and didn't tell you. Uh, Spooky's in my backpack."

"Spooky is in your backpack? Oh no! It's so hot today. Poor Spooky!"

"Yeah, that's what I was thinking."

"What are you going to do?"

"What am I going to do?" And your daughter starts having an internal dialogue trying to figure out this response: "Hey mom! This is when you get mad at me for being so irresponsible. I'm only 8 years old. You know you can't trust me with my life. You are going to have to blow off some steam, yell about all this, and then load us up in the Suburban and burn a bunch of expensive gas while we fix my mistakes."

"Yes, honey, what are you going to do?"

"Mom, I am eight. What can I do?"

"I don't know, sweetie."

"What is wrong with you, mom? Why are you acting so calm?"

"I don't know."

"Spooky is roasting on a bus somewhere, and all you have to say is 'I know' and 'I don't know'?"

"Probably so."

"This is far more serious than you seem to be taking it."

"That could be. Do you want my help with this?"

"Yes."

"Well, if this were my problem, I would probably start with the phone book and see if I could call someone at the place where they keep the buses. Would that be something you could try?"

"I am only eight. I don't know how to use a phone book."

"Oh no."

"Can you show me how?"

"I'd love to."

This lesson could lead to an adventure that includes learning that phone books make it difficult for most educated adults to find out how to call a school. There may be a lesson in how much it costs to have someone drive you around while you retrieve your hamster. A hamster is a pretty cheap lesson. Most of us are more interested in solving the immediate problem than we are in our children learning to take responsibility for their life. Don't worry, though, because if they don't learn it when they are children, they'll be coming to your house as adults. Then you will really be saying, "Oh no."

"No problem" is another *Love and Logic*® phrase that helps your child think for himself. It means, "No problem for me. But there's probably a problem coming up for you."

"I'm not going to do it! You can't make me!"

"No problem."

Remember, you need to be able to say this with a smile on your face. A smile can only be on the face of a person *who does not have a problem*. When our children are defiant or struggling with their problems, most of us do not wear a smile. Our faces say that we are people with a problem. This only works when you have "soft eyes" and a smile on your face. "No problem" also reminds us that in this situation, we are not the ones with the power to fix things. We need to convey this to our children: "It is your problem, so I will be back with you when you can think again. But right now, I can see that you are having an emotional seizure. I am not going to try to make you see or want what I want. I am going to wait and be with you when you are ready to take responsibility for this thing that only you have the power to solve."

BUILDING TRUST: MEAN WHAT YOU SAY

These are all great tools to help you protect the health and happiness of your garden. But once again, the best thing you can do to establish respectful boundaries with your children is to get good at telling yourself what to do and get out of the habit of telling others what to do. For many of us, it seems powerful, healthy, and righteous to bark out commands for our children to jump around and obey. We have this branded into our minds: "Our parents barked out orders. Everyone with power and authority in our lives all barked out orders. Isn't that what bosses do?"

Let's think about this. Is our goal as parents to coerce compliance from our children, or do we want something higher than that? By simply trying to get our kids to do what we want, we miss a golden opportunity—the opportunity to teach our children how to think for themselves, to problem solve, to make responsible choices both within and outside of our presence. Do we know what's going on in the heart of our child when we interact with them? Or are we just concerned that *"that sock ends up in that laundry basket!"* We get to decide.

When we bark out commands, we need to realize that we are really just trying to stop the rain. When we say to our kids, *"Don't you roll your eyes at me, young man!"* we are really saying, "Oh please, oh please, oh please, don't disobey me." When we say, "Get over here *right now!"* we had better follow it up with "Pretty please!" Because, once again, the fact is that we have zero power to enforce either one of those statements. What you do control—on a good day, remember—is you. You want to feel powerful? Tell your bones where to go, how long to stay there, what to put in your mouth and what not to let out of your mouth. If you want to feel powerless, try telling other people what to do. Try to get other people to do what you want them to do so you can be OK. Give them all the power over your well being. That is the recipe for a bad day. A great way to set healthy limits in our relationships is to get good at telling other people what we are going to do, and then letting them decide how they want to deal with that.

When we say what we mean, mean what we say, and do what we say we will do, then we are *trustworthy*. Our words mean something. But we weaken our words when we make threats or unenforceable statements such as, "Don't you talk to me like that!" or "You be nice to your brother!"

We also weaken our words when we spend a lot of time lecturing. I like to ask parents who lecture, "How's that working out for you?" I usually take a guess that it's not working. The point where you capture your child's attention and respect is not determined by how much noise you can fill the atmosphere with or how many words you can get out. It's determined by demonstrating that you meant what you said. That is what makes believers of your children. Remember Charlie Brown's schoolteacher? "Waa waa waa waa waa waa." That's what you sound like to a child who is not listening to you. The child says, "What? I am listening. Are you done? Can I go? I heard you!"

But oh no, you are not done: "Waa waa waa waa waa." You were impressed with your case—the points that you made, the analogies from your childhood that are relevant for today, and the fact that this was a golden opportunity to learn something. You don't even realize that you had no audience. If you want to make a difference, then get good at doing something and not just talking about something.

One of my favorite *Love and Logic*® stories is about a junior high principal who once had a great big problem. The junior high girls had discovered lipstick, and the bathroom mirrors had lip marks on them because the girls were trying to get the perfect lip print on the glass. The janitors were going nuts! They had to clean all these greasy mirrors in every girls' bathroom of the school every day. With the janitors ready to revolt, this principal decided to call an all-school assembly and make an announcement. She was going to show them a hammer.

So she gathered them in there and said, "Now hear this! Anyone who is caught pressing their lips on the mirrors of my school is going to regret the fact that their lips ever touched the glass. Are we communicating here? Am I clear?"

The boys were looking at each other, wondering how they could get their hands on some lipstick, because now they knew the way to make the principal go nuts. Well, the announcement didn't work. The problem just got worse. She mailed a newsletter to the parents of the students. That didn't work. She commissioned the school's toughest teacher to do his thing. That didn't work. Then she called Jim Fay, the founder of The *Love and Logic* Institute, to do his thing. He flew out to the school to meet with the principal.

Jim and the principal were standing in the hallway when a new custodian approached them and said, "Excuse me, but I couldn't help hearing that you are helping us out with the lipstick problem. Can I help?"

Jim Fay said, "Well, I haven't really come up with a solution just yet. But whatever you can do—take your best shot."

The custodian asked when the first break was, and the principal said 10:30. And so at 10:30 the custodian wheeled her cart into the girl's bathroom. She spun it around in a dramatic fashion so the girls would be sure to notice her. The custodian said, "Oh, excuse me." With all eyes watching, she grabbed a squeegee and a sponge, walked over to the toilet, splashed the sponge into the toilet and then slopped it up on the mirrors. The girls just stood there in disbelief as she ran the squeegee up and down the mirrors.

One by one the girls started screaming, "Eeew! What are you doing?"

The custodian turned to her. "What? I do it like this all the time!"

What was left to be said? What additional point could have been made to drive this home and teach them a lesson? Nothing. They just had some decisions to make.

Kids are really smart. They just need some good information to work with. You don't need too many words. Let your actions do most of the talking and teach them that when you say you are going to do something, you mean it. Follow through with what you say. I tell my kids, "You can do that if you want to, but I wouldn't." And they begin to think, "Why not?" It's not my job to take over their thinking. Yelling doesn't work for me. You can go ahead if you want, but I wouldn't.

POINTS TO PONDER:

1. How well have you understood the priority of taking care of yourself? What are some of the things that you do to handle stress, and how are they working out for you?

2. Which relational style do you relate to the most—passive or aggressive (or passive-

aggressive)? Do you need to make an adjustment in either valuing your own needs or the needs of others?

3. Do you find yourself barking out orders? Think of some scenarios in which you want your child's behavior to change and then create some statements that communicate what *you* are going to do.

4. Have you allowed your children to control you with the big red button of disrespect? How has this affected your connection with them?

5. What are some areas in the lives of your children where you might allow them to take more responsibility and to make more mistakes— places where the consequences aren't too expensive?

6. Are there areas of your children's behavior that you have tried to change through lecturing? If so, how can you create limits for your child in those areas by telling them what you are going to do and doing it?

Chapter 4

CHOICES

Now that we understand the priority of taking care of ourselves, we're going to look at our second responsibility as parents—empowering our kids. I've talked a little bit about setting limits with our children when it comes to "being fun." But there are many more skills we want our children to learn than simply how to control their tempers in our presence. We expose them to this real world of responsibility by offering choices—lots of choices. Remember, the earliest example we have is the scene in the Garden. God offered His kids choices. I wonder why?

In my workshops, I always do this particular exercise to demonstrate the deep human need for freedom and self-control. I usually do it when I've been with the audience an hour or so and have "marked" my victim. I pick the sweetest lady I can find. I ask her name, and then, while I am still in the front of the room I ask her, "How are you doing with me being this far away while I am talking?"

She'll say, "Fine."

I then walk right up next to her and say, "How about now?"

She will fidget and then say, "It's all right."

I then ask, "How about if I put my hands around your throat?"

The audience chuckles nervously and she says, "No, that would not be all right."

I then say, "What if I grab you off that chair, hold you down and won't let you up? What would you do?"

She says, "I would scream."

I say, "I am not letting go of you and no one in here can help you. What are you going to do?"

One time I was working with a lady named Sarah. We were at this point in the exercise and she asked, "You are not going to let go of me?"

I said, "No way."

"You're sure?"

"Yes ma'am."

Very matter-of-factly, she said, "Well, OK, I guess I would have to reach up over your arm and jam my thumb into your eye socket and touch your brain."

I dramatically jumped back, shrinking in mock terror from Sarah.

She giggled and said, "But you said that you weren't going to let go of me."

The audience roared with laughter.

Now, how did I take sweet Sarah and turn her into a homicidal, brain-touching maniac? I simply did not respect her need for control—self-control. With each step, I threatened her ability to control herself, until she was in a panic. She was willing to hurt me and in this case, kill me. Was this because she is so mean and rebellious? No, it was because she must have her freedom. If she must hurt me to regain her self-control, then she will make that choice.

One day when Levi was about 3 years old, Sheri had to wake him up from his nap, get him dressed, and load him in the car so she could pick up Brittney, who was waiting at school. It was snowing outside, so she had to bundle him up and put his boots on. He was still groggy from his nap and immediately began to struggle with her hand, which had his ankle and was trying to force it into the boot. Sheri realized that the struggle needed to move from his foot and her hand to between his left and right ear. So she asked, "Levi, do want to take your teddy bear or leave it here?"

"Huh?"

"Do you want to take your teddy bear or leave it here?"

"Take it."

Then he relaxed and she put both feet in the boots, allowed her to dress him, and off they went. He needed some control in the relationship, and she knew that she could offer him a remedy for his deep needs as a human being. Yes, children really are people. And if we fail to honor the truth that *the only person who can control you is you* when we interact with our children, we are inviting them to prove it to us. If you say, "Get over here right now," even a compliant child can demonstrate to you that you don't control her. She simply dictates the speed at which she complies. That's when we start reaching for hammers, for ways to intimidate our kids in order to convince them that we do control them. But it's a lie, and as long as it guides your actions, you will keep manufacturing ways to convince people to give their self-control to you. When you do, you effectively train your children to be controlled by angry, aggressive people or whiny, manipulative people, and to try to control others in the same way.

When we give our children choices, we validate them by recognizing that they need power in their relationship with us. If we act like we have all the power and they have none when they're little, it sets us up for a pretty rough transition when they're older and it's time to share the power. In our children's adolescence, we can mistakenly figure these power struggles are about respect and their value for us as parents more than about our kids needing self-control. In our panic to preserve our status in the relationship, we end up getting so crazy that we blurt out, "I did offer you a couple choices. Do you want to live or die? Do you want to be buried in our yard or the neighbor's yard?" We need to start sharing the power with them from early on in the relationship.

Like the one-liners, offering choices needs to become something that is second nature to you, because you will need to be able to do it under pressure—usually the pressure of your children's *poor choices*. You often need to be able to respond pretty quickly to those. If your child stepped in doggy doo and then came in the house, would you say, "Oh look, doggy doo on your foot. Oh, honey, stop. Oh, um, could you, oh, um, would you, oh, um…"? You need to present some choices. This would be a great time to be ready to say, "You can stand outside with those shoes like that or you can figure out a way to keep the doo out of our house. Take your time." Thus, it's to your benefit to practice offering choices as often as you can, even when it doesn't seem necessary, so that it becomes habitual. It may look something like this:

"Hey, you going to the store with me or you staying here?"

"Yeah, I am going."

"You want to ride in the front seat or the back seat?"

"Dad, it's just me that's riding with you!"

"I know. Do you want to go into the store with me or stay out here?"

"Dad, we are buying shoes for me! Why are you acting so weird?"

"I don't know," with a great big smile across your face.

Practicing helps you be ready for "game day." Believe it or not, this is one of the sticking points for many parents trying to make the change to another style of leading their kids. They cannot think of two choices when faced with a power struggle. All that comes to mind is "Do you want to do what I said or...do what I said?"

We share control by offering choices. Now, there are times when you need to say something like, "Get out of the road!" Obviously, at that point you shouldn't be offering any choices. "You want your blood inside or outside your body?" That consequence is way too expensive to let them learn from their poor choices. But this type of commando style cannot be the general operating system of the relationship. If it is, then you probably have an extremely high level of anxiety between you two and likely a fragile connection. Learning to master the art of offering good choices will bolster an empowering culture in your home. At the same time, it sets you up for success when you need to set limits for their behavior, such as:

"Hey, do you want to speak respectfully while you are so upset or do you want to talk about this in an hour?"

"Are you tired or do you need something to do?"

"Everyone at this dinner table is fun to be around. Are you ready to be fun or were you going to go somewhere else until you are fun?"

THREE GUIDELINES FOR CHOICES

There are basically three guidelines for setting limits with choices. I derived these guidelines from the *Becoming a Love and Logic Parent* materials. First of all, I want you to notice something about the choices I just offered. In each case, either option I laid out was something that I could be happy for my child to choose. We give our children *real choices* when we show them two ways to get something done and either way is fine with us. If we offer our child a choice between what we want them to do and what we don't want them to do, then we set them up to choose poorly just to feel powerful. We can empower them to make good choices by offering two powerful choices. You want to give choices where either choice is great for you. "Do you want to do what I say, or do you want me to spank you?" is not a good choice, because one of those does not make you happy, and any kid that is trying to win a power struggle will choose the second option: "Spank me.

Go ahead. Make my day." "Do you want to clean your room or pay me to do it for you?" is an empowering set of choices because you can be happy with either outcome.

The second guideline for offering good choices is that you have to make sure that your child understands the choices being offered. When you tell them to clean their rooms, for example, you need to know that the picture of the completed job in their mind matches the one in yours. Have you ever told your kid to clean her room, only to have her go in there and come out eight seconds later? And when she did, you said, "No way! I saw that room. There is no way you cleaned that in eight seconds."

"Oh yeah, I did!" she replied. "I kicked a path to the laundry basket. That's what you wanted, right?"

We have to go through the task step by step to show them what a clean room looks like to us. In carrying out this instruction, I encourage you to ask questions, which are like choices, because questions cause kids to think instead of simply absorbing information:

"Well, what do you think about the bed? Is it messy or neat?"

"Neat? Do you mean like the pillow should be on it?"

"Sure. Now, what do you think about the bedspread? Should it be on top, or underneath?

"On it? Like you do it?"

"Yeah!"

"This is going to take me a year!"

"Probably so. What do you think about the floor? Do you think it is picked up and vacuumed?"

"*And vacuumed*! That's not fair!"

"I know."

"You know it's not fair?"

"Well, probably so. And how about the garbage can—full or empty?"

"Empty."

"And how about the clothes bag—full of dirty clothes or full of clean clothes?"

"Well what do you want me to do with the clean clothes? Put them away?"

"Probably so. Any questions?"

"What, did you read some parenting book or something?"

"Yep."

"Well, it's not going to work on me!"

"I know."

Now, here's the final guideline for offering choices. This is the point where most parents don't know what to do. You've given your children a choice where either outcome is great, and you've made sure they understand the task at hand. But the thing is, when you offer a kid a choice between A or B, any kid with a brain is going to say, "C." How do you get them to stick with either A or B? This is where you need to have a plan—a plan to enforce your choices with consequences.

Let's keep with the room-cleaning scenario. You walk into your kid's room and ask, "Hey, would you like to clean your room or pay me to do it for you?" When you offer this choice, any kid with a brain will ask, "How much?" You might think, "That's disrespectful! I can't believe you just popped off with that. You're supposed to choose the first one." But that's not disrespect, that's wisdom. If you take the car to the mechanic and say, "Hey, will you fix this?" and they say, "Sure," you had better ask, "How much?"

So your kid says, "I could hire someone to do this? Great. How much?"

"Fifty bucks." (That's how much I would charge. Maybe you'd do it for five. But you set the price. It's your market.)

"Fifty bucks! Have you been drinking?"

"Probably so."

"I'm not paying you fifty bucks."

"No problem." And you say it with a smile on your face. Remember what "No problem" means? "No problem for me, but it's probable that a problem is coming for you."

"I'm not going to do it. You can't make me!"

"Not a problem. I'll know what you have decided in ten minutes." And off you go. Where do you go? Well, first you go pray. You go pray that your kid doesn't clean his room. "Oh Holy One of Israel, please, if you love me, hold him back. Prevent him, oh Mighty God, from getting off that bed and taking responsibility right now. Cover his eyes and let him fall into this hole, that he may learn that I am a force to be reckoned with and have the abilities to set limits in my house. I so want to present him with this amazing consequence. Oh please, turn my words from trash into truth, Mighty God." You pray that your kid makes a poor choice because then you get to do the stuff. If you can do that, then you know you're ready. You need that kind of faith.

After you pray, you get the shovel, flamethrower, tetanus shot, and whatever else you need to go in and do a good job. When the ten minutes are up you are standing in the doorway and there he is sitting on the bed with his iPod on, absolutely ignoring you, just as you have prayed. You bring the cleaning stuff in and start going at it. When you're done, the room looks just like you want it—an extra bonus!

As you're leaving, you hear, "I'm not paying you." You, smiling, march out of the room. The kid goes, "That was weird. Whatever."

You think, "Oh Jesus, you are good to me."

In a little while, after he's had time to forget that you cleaned his room for him, you bump into your son in the hall and say, "Hey, I was wondering, how do you want to settle that whole room thing? I take Visa, MasterCard, American Express, cash, and hard labor." It's kind of fun to do this, because there's no anger. There's been no power struggle, so he isn't aware that you're reeling him in.

"I said I wasn't going to pay you. It's unfair that you came into my room. I didn't invite you. I did not sign a contract. I'll get a lawyer if I have to."

And you say, "No problem. I'll know by the time you go to school tomorrow what you've decided. I'm certain that I can get fifty dollars for your Xbox on eBay, or maybe from your brother. Or the neighbor—then you can go to his house and play it. He's over here a lot. I think he likes it. Or I'm sure I can get fifty bucks for your CD collection or your video games. I'm sure I can get fifty bucks for something. Don't you worry about it, though."

When you tell somebody who's trying to be oppositional not to worry, what does he do? He worries. And he should worry, because you are the IRS. You are a force to be reckoned with. You are the ruler of the house, and you are kind about it and you're gentle. But your child is about to learn the truth about you.

"I will worry if I want to. You would never do that."

"Probably so."

Now don't you dare offer this—don't even start it—if you are not willing to sell that Xbox, and I don't mean put it in the cupboard for a couple months until he is sorry. *Do not act this powerful if you are not going to follow through, because you will teach your child not to believe a word you say*. And don't do this if you're mad. Only do this if you're happy, if you can say, "Oh, please do it. Make four poor choices in a row. These are some of the best consequences you will ever experience."

You may be thinking, "Wow, isn't that kind of extreme? I don't know. I couldn't do that unless I was mad. How do you do it with a smile on your face? Is this like an evil spirit?" No, this is fun, because your kid is learning a powerful lesson about personal responsibility and the consequences of his choices. The next time you say, "Hey, you want to clean that room or do you want to pay me to do it for you?" he will say, "Get away from my room!" (He will also probably start hiding his stuff.)

And as for it being extreme, let me remind you that this is how the world works. Are you tired of paying taxes? Why don't you just say, "I am not paying these taxes anymore"? You don't say it because the IRS will say, "No problem. Would you like to change your mind or would you like to come to the auction?" The IRS has the power to govern, to set limits. It has the power to enforce consequences because it is a real force. No one from the IRS will come to you and say, "Oh no, you don't. Yes, you will. You had better change your mind." The IRS is not afraid that you are going to make poor choices. *It just knows what it is going to do.* The IRS is going to sell your Xbox.

This is the real world, and it really works like this. We are all making choices in every situation, and those choices are bringing certain consequences into our lives. When we show our children what the real world is like, we equip them to be aware of the fact that they are making choices all the time and we enable them to take responsibility for them. Their ability to think and problem solve is activated as they learn to ask, "How did that work out for me?" And they get to do it before the consequences are too expensive. Fifty bucks is nothing when you think about the pit of debt most kids are digging themselves into when they leave home and discover the world of credit cards.

WAKE UP CALLS AND REFEREES

One of the limits we had to set with Levi was getting up on time. Ever since they were tiny, Taylor didn't need much sleep at all, but Levi needed lots of sleep. When they shared a room as little boys, we would hear Levi say, "Taylor, stop talking to me." The kid just needed some sleep. And when we got him up in the morning, he was a sloth. So I told him, "Hey, buddy, the first wake up call is free, because I love you. I supply a free wake-up call." What does that imply? There could be a second one coming to you. But don't you worry, because at ten bucks a pop, I will be sure to do a great job waking you up. I take all the covers off and say, "Hey, how you doing, buddy?" I clap, flick the light, and give him kisses. "Love you, love you, love you, love you. Hey, I get ten bucks for this." In the course of Levi's life and his big challenge with getting up, I have made thirty dollars.

When sibling rivalry erupts, many parents intervene with, "Knock it off! Stop it! You be nice to your brother." But you can't do anything about that. Here's an idea. Say, "Hey, it's obvious that you guys need a referee to make sure nobody gets blood on mom's furniture. I charge ten bucks apiece. Ding!" The first time they might not stop, and your prayers are answered. By the second time, they'll probably say, "No," and just walk away. Unless your other child starts slapping and biting himself and throwing himself on the floor, it's over.

Sheri and I offered lots of services in our home, just like in America. In America, you don't have to cook dinner anymore. Somebody else will cook dinner for you. Cha-ching. You don't have to iron shirts, wash clothes, or do any of that anymore. Somebody else will do it for you. Cha-ching. It's the American way. We might as well prepare our children to live in this world. We simply said, "If you'd like it, let me know. It's your problem and your life to manage. It's my service to provide. I decide if it's free or if it costs. But we have lots of services. We have a room-cleaning service. We have a wake-up service. We have a light-in-your-room management service. We have a chore-swap service." Once again, it's your market. You get to come up with creative ways to introduce your children to responsibility, power, and freedom in the real world. Remember, our children must experience the weight of their freedom. God intends for His children to know how to manage high levels of freedom.

CHICKEN COOP OR TRASH SHED?

Speaking of the "chore-swapping service," I want to tell you one of my favorite stories in the world. It's a story about my 14-year-old daughter when we lived in Weaverville. For whatever reason, Brittney did not share Sheri's conviction about dishes being done every night. Brittney thought dishes should be done on occasion—special occasions, like Thanksgiving. And so, periodically, I would hear Sheri saying, "Brittney! Did you get those dishes done?"

And Brittney would say, "I am! I'm going to!"

A little while later, "Brittney, did you get the dishes done?"

"What? I am in the bathroom!"

Later, "Brittney, don't go to bed without getting those dishes done."

"I wasn't going to. I am doing my homework!"

The next morning, "Brittney, you didn't get those dishes done."

"*Uh*! I didn't have time!"

And day after day they had this thing going on with the dishes. One Saturday morning Brittney didn't get the dishes done, and her friend Rebecca came over. They hung out for a while, and then, poof! They disappeared. They went to Rebecca's house. Sheri looked at me, and flames literally started to come out of the top of her head.

I said, "Honey, you look a little upset."

"She doesn't respect me! This happens over and over! *You!* You do something!"

So I ran in and did the dishes. It was about a four-minute chore. A little while later, Brittney and Rebecca came in, all dolled up. Brittney said, "Mom! Dad! Rebecca's mom is taking us to the city. Can I go?"

I said, "Brittney, I did your dishes for you."

She said, "*Uh*! Dad! I was going to do them!"

"I know."

"Dad, that's not fair!"

"Probably not. What would you like to do for me, the trash shed or the chicken coop?"

She asked, "Can I look?"

"Sure you can, sweetie."

In Weaverville we didn't have a garbage collection service. We had to take our trash to the dump ourselves. So I had an 8′8′10 shed, and I knew it was time to go to the dump when I saw trash in the window of the door. By then you couldn't even find a garbage can in there. Brittney went out and opened the shed door. Flies immediately swarmed out and started hitting her in the face.

"Oh, gross! Gross!"

Rebecca asked, "What are you doing? Are you in trouble? How do you know you're in trouble? No one is even yelling at you!"

Brittney headed to the chicken coop, opened the pen and started kicking at the chickens. "Stupid chickens! Get out of the way!" Then she came back into the house and said, "Chicken pen."

I said, "Thank you. Would you like to do that today or tomorrow after church?"

"I can do this tomorrow?"

"If you want."

"Can I go to town today?"

"If you want."

"Dad!" She gave me a big hug because she was going to clean the chicken pen for me the next day. It was a beautiful thing. And off they went.

Now, this is the part where most parents are so indignant. "What! Are you kidding me? You let a sinner go? Don't you know that there must be a blood sacrifice for the atoning of sin?" Hang with me for a few more minutes and you'll see the genius in all this. Oh, and by the way, that was the old covenant that required the blood sacrifice.

The next day we got home from church and it was pouring rain. Why? Because Jesus loves me! I said, "Hey Britt, remember that little deal we have going on? I was just wondering, do you want to wear my rain jacket or that pretty sweater?"

"The rain jacket."

"Do you want to wear my rubber boots or those shiny shoes?"

"Your boots."

"Do you want to use the shovel or the pitchfork?"

She said, "Well, I'll probably need both!" And off she went. *Three hours later* she came in looking like Homeless Hannah. She was dragging both tools back toward the house and had straw hanging off her head.

I said, "Sweetie, thank you!"

She flipped her soaking wet hair off her face and said, "Whatever!" She then went off to take a shower.

A few days later I heard Sheri say, "Brittney! Get those dishes done!"

Brittney said, "I will!"

I said, "I'll get it!"

The next second, Brittney came *flying* into the kitchen and said, "*Get away from my dishes!*"

Consequences breed ownership, and ownership breeds responsibility. Those were her dishes, and I'd better keep my stinking chicken coop. What did this lesson enforce in my daughter's thinking? Well, it enforced the truth that in the home, just as in the real world, we all have responsibilities, and that it's in our best interest for each of us to make a contribution to the health and happiness of this little economy. She also learned that these responsibilities, just as in the real world, are time-sensitive. They set limits for us, and we are making choices within these limits all the time, whether those choices are proactive or passive. Ignoring responsibility is as much a choice as taking it.

WHO'S GOT THE PROBLEM?

Offering choices and enforcing consequences guides our children progressively toward taking ownership for their lives, their choices, their responsibilities, and their problems. Clearly, it requires wisdom and courage for you to discern the areas of responsibility that your children are prepared to handle and then to entrust them with those responsibilities. It also takes wisdom and courage to guide your children through experiencing the consequences of their choices. There are two types of parental intervention we want to avoid in order to do this successfully. The first type of intervention is swooping into the situation and fixing the problem, and the second is presenting a consequence mixed with anger and punishment.

Swooping in to fix your child's problem effectively prevents him or her from taking ownership for it. I remember a couple who came to me after one of my *Love and Logic*® parenting workshops. The mother said, "We've got a big problem at home. Our kids are trying to kill each other. They hurt each other all of the time, and I'm constantly pulling them apart."

I said, "Oh no."

She said, "Yeah, I quit my job so that I could be home when they get home from school."

The dad said, "And I'm not quitting my job."

I said, "Let me ask you something. Are your children hunting down other children and trying to kill them?"

"No."

"Okay, then you probably have regular kids who fight in the safety of their parents' presence. You need to introduce them to the idea that this is their problem."

Now, this mom had never seen another person's problem before in her whole life. She felt like they were all hers. The dad asked, "Do you mean they should punch it out?"

I said, "I don't know."

They went home, walked in the door, and sat on the couch, a little scared. But they thought they were ready. The 8-year-old came out of his room and walked right into the 11-year-old's room. Arguments, pushing, and slapping ensued. He came down the hallway and looked at his parents, crying. He said, "Mommy, I didn't touch him. I was just standing there, and he hit me for no reason."

She said, "Oh no."

He said, "Oh no?" His internal dialogue said, "You understand, this is the time that you jump off the couch, run down there, and kick his behind. We've got this little power structure going on here." He asked, "You're going to do nothing? You're just going to sit there?"

She said, "I don't know."

He asked, "You don't know? What, are you stupid? Are you nuts?" Any kid worth keeping can run their parents through a couple sets of these exercises. He was looking for buttons to push.

She said, "Probably so."

"Well, that sucks. You suck."

"I know."

"You know? Fine. You love him more than you love me. I know you do. You always have."

"Nice try."

"Mommy, nice try? What's the matter with you people? I hate you. I hate both of you."

And he turned around and ran back into the 11-year-old's room, who immediately said, "Get out of my room!" So he came back out, looked at his parents, then went into his room and began to rip it apart, smashing his toys. Mom and Dad were still sitting on the couch, wondering if this boy was going to need counseling. Eventually, things settled down and the parents went and opened the door to his room. He was lying sideways across his bed, fully dressed and asleep. Dad shook his head and headed for bed. Mom put the blanket over him and headed for bed. At two in the morning she woke up at and heard her son groaning. She came into his room and asked, "Honey, what's the matter?"

He said, "My throat hurts." So she went and got a cool cloth and a lozenge. When she came back he said, "Mom, I don't really hate you."

She said, "I know, honey. I love you. Good night."

First thing in the morning, the boy came down the hallway. His mom was cooking breakfast and his dad was with her. The dad and the boy caught each other's eye and the boy put his head down and walked toward the dad, who met him in the hallway. They held each other for a moment. Then Dad said, "Smell that breakfast?"

His son said, "Smells good."

He said, "Do you want some?"

He said, "Yeah, I'm hungry."

"You can have all the breakfast you want as soon as you get that room cleaned up. Take your time."

"Have you seen my room?"

"Oh yeah. Love you."

And he went off to deal with his problem.

Any kid with a brain is not going to take you giving them back their problem lying down. It's going to be put back in your lap as fast as he can put do so, because he feels totally unequipped to deal with it. It's a natural reaction, so don't go through the exercises of setting limits and then jump over and grab that problem and take it back.

Be aware that your kid is quite likely to run you through a knothole in the process of transferring the problem, especially if you have had an agreement in the past that this problem of theirs Pull out your *Love and Logic*® one-liners and stand your ground. The next step will be to play the victim. "You don't love me," or "He always gets what he wants," are some of the ways to get parents to defend themselves from the accusation of being an unfair person. And finally, rejection is sometimes the toughest tactic to handle. "I hate you!" is never something you want to hear from your child's lips, but kids know that desperate times call for desperate measures.

Your children's negative reaction to responsibility is usually *not* a sign that they are incapable or unprepared to handle it. The fact that they just made a mess by showing disrespect when they were confronted with responsibility is another issue, which we will discuss in the following chapter. The point here is that you can't afford to be so concerned about your kids cleaning up their messes that you don't allow them to make them in the first place.

When they do, the first priority is not cleaning it up, but making sure the mess has an owner. *Every problem must find its owner before we can ever offer a solution.* If you try to solve another human being's problem when that person doesn't have a problem, you are not being helpful. You are a nag. You are a meddler. You are a manipulator. That is the truth. You can say, "No, I'm not. I'm just trying to be a good mom. I'm just trying to be a good dad. I'm just loving you." But that is because you are still operating from a paradigm where love looks like control.

Imagine that there is a car in a parking lot and somebody sets its alarm off. It refuses to stop, and everyone around you starts going, "What can we do?" You need to find the owner, the person who has the little thing on his key chain. If you bust a window out of that car and yank the wires, you're in big trouble. "I was just solving the problem." It wasn't yours to solve. The only way you can solve another person's problem is through violation. That's what happens in our relationships when we have not found the owner of a problem but are determined to solve it anyway.

How do you know when something is your child's problem? Well, one way to know is simply by asking yourself, "If I do nothing, what will happen to me?" If the answer is, "Nothing," then you have discovered that it is not yours. If you do nothing about your child's messy room, what will happen to you? If you do nothing about her grades, what will happen to you? Whose problem is your fifth grader's homework? We all know the right answer, but some of us have blood pressure problems at home when our kids are not getting their homework done, because we've been trained that our children's problems are ours.

Of course, as a parent you also need to ask the next question, which is, what will happen to my child if she mishandles her problem? That's where you have to judge how expensive the consequences are and leave room for your child to make a poor choice, just like God did in the Garden. This is where we must make sure that love drives out fear, for we rightly recognize that we are taking a risk by allowing our children to experience some potentially painful consequences. But we cannot falsely protect our children from consequences in the name of love. Otherwise, our kids learn that their problems are not theirs but are really someone else's.

Some consequences are absolutely unaffordable. When life or death or serious physical harm is in the balance, we waive the choice and rush in. But, the rest of the times, although sometimes difficult to watch, are powerful learning opportunities.

One day, when Brittney was in fourth grade, Sheri said, "I am not making lunches for fourth graders anymore. I bought you some stuff and there is the lunch pail, so have at it." Brittney was excited, because she likes to be in charge of stuff. The next morning she got all her goodies in her lunch box, and we left for school. I dropped her off, came home, walked in the house, and what was on the counter? The lunch box.

Sheri said, "She's going to call."

I said, "I know."

"You're going to answer it."

The phone rang and Sheri was standing right there. To me she said, "Chicken!" and then picked up the phone. "Hello."

Brittney said, "Mom. This is Brittney."

"I could tell by the way you called me 'Mom.' What's going on?"

"Mom, I forgot my lunch."

Sheri said, "Oh no. Forgot your lunch."

"Mom, it's sitting right there on the counter right by the bread box there."

"I know. I see it. It's purple, huh?

"Yeah, that's the one. Mom, can you bring me my lunch?"

"I'm sorry Britt, but I'm not going to the school today."

"Mom, oh no. Come on, please?"

Sheri asked, "What are you going to do, Britt?" If you ask another human being, "What are you going to do?" it infers that the problem is something you can do nothing about.

"What am I going to do? Well, I was going to call you and have you come and bring my lunch."

"Probably so. So what are you going to do today? What else can you try?"

"Uh..."

Sheri said, "I've got a couple of ideas if you would like to hear them."

Brittney asked, "You are not going to bring me my lunch?"

"I'm sorry, Britt, I'm not going to the school. I have a couple of ideas if you would like to hear them."

"What?"

Sheri said, "Some kids dig around in the trash and see what's left in the trash after everybody is gone. How will that work out for you?"

Brittney said, "That's a stupid idea."

Sheri said, "Yeah. I've got another idea."

"Is it better than the last one?"

"Probably so."

"What?"

"Well, some kids ask their friends to share their lunch with them. How will that work out for you?"

"I don't want to ask anybody for a lunch. I want the lunch I made. It's got the Twinkies in it."

"I know. I've got one more idea. It's all I have." See, one of the great things about not having a problem to solve is that you don't have to come up with all the ideas. You are not solving it; you're just helping.

"What?"

"Some people go to the lady that sits at the front desk and ask, 'What do we do at school if we forget our lunch?'"

Brittney said, "I don't want to talk to that lady. I don't know her."

"Okay. Well, Britt, I know you will get this solved. You are a very smart girl. I love you very much. Goodbye."

Ugh! That was hard to do. We only lived a few blocks from the school. My wife could have ended it all with a quick trip to the school office. But instead, she allowed Britt to own the problem and created an opportunity for her to solve it. Sheri was a bit nervous that she was in trouble with Brittney when she got home that day from school. Waiting for a few moments, trying to feel Britt's mood, she asked, "How was lunch today, sweetheart?"

"Lunch?" Britt muttered, seeming to have forgotten about it, "Oh, I shared Olivia's lunch with her today."

Wow! This child is a genius. She actually found a way to put food in her stomach when she was hungry.

Now, most of us won't go through that kind of torture when we have a child on the other end going, "Help! Help!" We have the capability to go marching to the school and say, "Here is your lunch. Here is your permission slip. Here is your jacket. Here is your backpack. Here is your head." It just seems like it is going to be easier and more loving to fix it for them. But in the end, it's to your benefit and theirs to communicate a message like this: "Honey, I love you and believe in you, and therefore I want you to find out that you are capable of solving this problem."

The message is clear: "I can't control you. I can't control your appetite. I can't control your study habits. I can't control your respect. I can't control the tongue in your mouth. I can't control your attitude. I can't control anything of yours. I can set some limits. I've got some pretty cool tools to use when you mess up, but I need you to learn quickly that your side of our relationship is yours. Your life is yours and you've got to learn how to use it, because there is coming a day when I won't be around."

Adults have many options in how they will solve life's problems. We want to offer our children an experience of the real world adults live in while they are still in our homes. Teaching them to think and problem solve comes through allowing them to create solutions outside of what we would decide for them. It can be difficult to trust them with this latitude of freedom, but it prepares them for the world they will enter one day as adults.

SAD OR MAD?

The other thing that *Love and Logic*® teaches in presenting consequences, besides preventing children from experiencing them by fixing the problem, is letting anger and punishment get mixed up in the presentation. Anger and punishment are destructive for two reasons—they distract your children from learning, and they damage your connection with them.

Imagine that you're driving down the road. You look in your rearview mirror and see red lights flashing. You hope that they are chasing somebody else, but you pull over and the cop goes with you. Your heart sinks. He walks up to the car, raps on your window and says, "Get out of the car." You don't move right away, so he grabs your door handle, reaches in, and grabs you by the shirt. He starts yanking you out of your seat belt. He says, "Get out of the car. I can't believe people like you are driving on my highway. Come here." He reaches in, undoes your seat belt, grabs you, pulls you out, and throws you up against the car. Now, what are you thinking? Are you thinking about your poor choice to drive over the speed limit? No. You're thinking, "I wonder if I can get his gun. Who is this loser? Idiot. What's your problem? I wasn't even speeding. Jerk. I'm taking you to court."

When someone gets angry about your mistake, his or her anger diverts your focus from dealing with the poor choice you made to the problem you're having with that person—to your need to defend yourself. It attacks, weakens, and destroys connection between two people. Anger is your enemy, even passive-aggressive anger—the Christian kind of anger. Passive-aggressive anger is expressed in cutting sarcasm or criticism, rejection, or withholding love. When you choose a passive-aggressive response to your child's failure, when you choose to withhold love because his or her performance has fallen, it is still anger. It is still punishment, and it's attacking your connection. So, unless you want your kids to disconnect from you and spend their time figuring out how to protect themselves from you, you will want to work hard to eliminate anger from your interactions with them.

Instead, you want to be able to offer sadness when your child makes a mistake. What would happen, for example, if the cop handled the same situation very differently and without the use of anger? Say that he walks up to you and waits until you roll your window down. He asks, "Can I see your license, registration, and proof of insurance please?"

You say, "Sure—here is my license and registration. Where did I put that proof of insurance? Oh, here it is."

"Do you know what the speed limit is here? It's 65. I had you clocked at 87. If you would care to come and look, I have it on the radar still."

"No, that's OK. I just wasn't paying attention. I was just talking on my cell phone. Sorry."

"I'll be right back." He goes back to see if you have escaped from some Texas prison or something, and then comes back with his little pad. In the neatest handwriting imaginable, he tells you that this is not a confession or an admission of guilt. It is just a promise to appear, and he has cited you for 85 in a 65 zone, because he is a generous guy. You sign it. He tears off a piece and hands it to you. You say, "Thank you." The he suggests a couple more options. You might pay the fine as soon as you get it, or you could appear and contest this ticket on this day, or you might check into taking some classes to reduce the impact to your insurance. He asks if you understand, and you say yes. Then he says, "Slow it down. Be safe." And you say, "Thank you," again. He walks away from your car. You put your blinker on, get back onto the road, and off you go.

And as you're driving down the road, this molasses-type material is floating down over your head and it's called "consequences." You're thinking, "Oh my gosh. I got a ticket. I can't believe I got a ticket. This is going to cost a million dollars. When was the last ticket I got? I can't think. My insurance. Sheri is going to kill me. That was our vacation money." It's all just dripping. And you're driving the speed limit.

Remember, consequences are some of the best teachers. And sadness and empathy help to keep the focus on the real problem, the poor choice, while sending the message that you care about the person who made it. But anger violates and sabotages the very goals that you most desire for your children when they fail—not only that they learn from their mistakes, but also that they can lean into their relationship with their parents as a source of wisdom and comfort as they go through that learning process.

Sadness and empathy are what the Holy Spirit shows us when we fail. He doesn't punish us. He comforts us. He shows us that He is sad for us, and invites us to come, of our own free will, to benefit from His great wisdom and power for fixing problems. (See, for example, John 14:26; John 16: 13; Gal. 4:6.) His response to our failure actually helps us to trust Him more. And when we respond to our children like He responds to us, they trust us more because they learn that they can fail in front of us.

Jesus provides us an awesome example of creating a safe place for those who fail (John 8:1-11). When a woman was caught in the very act of adultery (I always wonder what they did with the man), the Pharisees brought her before Jesus. They knew that the Law required that she be killed for her sins. This was a ploy to show the people that Jesus was trapped by the same "Yellow truck/Red truck" mentality that they were. The Pharisees thought they had Jesus pinned to his own rules for sinners. But, in one fell swoop, Jesus disarmed their attempt and displayed a power far superior to punishment: love.

Neither does the Holy Spirit withdraw from us or threaten to punish us when we fail. Withholding our love is something that perhaps more of us are tempted to do with our kids than to blow up, and I think dads tend to have a bigger struggle with this than moms. At one point when Brittney was in sixth grade, she was getting poor grades. When we finally got a progress report, I said, "Whoa! Hey, why were you hiding this?" She said, "I was afraid that if you knew, you wouldn't love me anymore, Dad." That was a revelation for me. Remember, I spanked Britt at every turn for failing up until she was about 8 years old. My frustration and anger at her failure to comply left an impression in her mind even now, four years later. She expected me to give and withhold love on the basis of her behavior. I was now trying to do a really good job of sending her the vibe that she was loved unconditionally, but I recognized that still at times there would be this twinge of disappointment when my kids failed, and I wouldn't go clean up the mess. I would just avoid it, or they would see that I was angry. That was a little "Oh no, how's that working out for you?" for me, so I started working on it a little harder.

Psalm 46:1-2 says, "God is our refuge and strength, an ever-present help in trouble. Therefore we will not fear though the earth give way and the mountains fall into the heart of the sea" (NIV). It is vital, when we present our children with the consequences of their poor choices, that we show them that we are sad for them and are going to be there with them as they work through finding the solutions to their problems.

It's the key to protecting the heart of the matter in all of this—the *connection*. The limits we set with our children will show them what the real world is like, but it is our heart connection with them, our love, that will motivate them to embrace the journey of responsibility and growth before them. Building and protecting that heart connection is what we will focus on in the next chapter.

POINTS TO PONDER:

1. Do you give your child real choices, or do you make them choose between what you want them to do and punishment?

2. Do you struggle with allowing your children to experience the consequences of their choices? Why is it more loving to comfort your children as they experience painful consequences than to keep them from experiencing them?

3. What are some of your children's problems, if any, that you have taken on as your own?

4. Why is it disrespectful to solve another person's problem for him or her?

5. Do you have a hard time working through your own anger or disappointment when your child fails? What are some things you can do to enable you to draw near to him or her with empathy and sadness as he or she picks up the pieces?

Chapter 5

PROTECTING AND BUILDING HEART CONNECTIONS

"It was for freedom that Christ set us free...For you were called to freedom, brethren; only do not turn your freedom into an opportunity for the flesh, but through love serve one another" (Galatians 5:1,13 NASB).

Throughout this book I have tried to show you the nature and importance of freedom. As I stated at in the first chapter, we were all created to be free, and God paid the highest price He could pay to restore that freedom to us after it was lost. But once again, freedom is only important because it is an essential requirement of the greater purpose for which we were created: love. Because love is the whole purpose for freedom, freedom is destroyed when we use it for anything else. It's like plugging a toaster in a socket with a completely different voltage pumping through it than it was made to use. Unless we are using our free-dom to love God and one another, we simply won't be able to walk in freedom and cultivate an environment of freedom around us. And we won't be able to love one another well and cultivate healthy relationships if we are not working to protect and honor each person's responsibility of self-control, which is the heart of freedom.

The same summer Levi went to public high school, he joined the football team. It was September, and we got to go to the games and watch him play. The freshmen played on Thursday evenings and the junior varsity and varsity played on Friday evenings. About the third weekend into the season, he came home from practice and said, "Coach wants us to all be at the varsity game this week so we can see how they run the plays. Can I go to the football game on Friday night?"

I looked at Sheri and could see the same feelings I was having. We were both remembering what we did at football games. And it had nothing to do with the football game. So, I said to him, "Son, I am scared, but you can go."

"I can go! Awesome!" He bolted from the room.

The game was an "away game," so I drove to the next town to pick him up. There he was, right were he said he'd be. As he loaded his stuff into the truck, I was hoping not to smell anything that would make this a really long night. He was clean. We got home, pulled into the driveway, and parked the truck. When we got out and headed for the house, he reached over and touched my arm and said, "Dad, thanks for trusting me."

I said, "You are welcome, son. Thanks for protecting us."

He said, "You are welcome, Dad."

This young man knows that he has a responsibility for half of a relationship. His half. He knows that no one manages his half but him. He's been trained to believe that and his life shows that he is taking responsibility for his half of "us."

If we are going to train our children to handle freedom as the priority of relationship, then we need to do our best to help our kids make a strong connection between these two messages: "I love you very much," and "What are you going to do?" When we tie choices, questions, and limits to the message of love, our kids learn that those are essential aspects of learning to manage their end of a relationship for which we have a very high value. They learn that managing their freedom is what cultivates and protects a respectful, loving connection with us. Our desire as parents should be that their value for that connection becomes the thing that directs them in the choices they make. We especially desire this for them because ultimately, the way that God intends for them to be governed is by their value for their connection with Him.

As I have mentioned, our kids can learn to relate to us in the mode of offering and making choices from the time they are very young. One of our family home movies is useful for proving this point. When our kids were tiny, Sheri started the tradition of making a Christmas video where the kids would say, "Hi dad, we love you! Merry Christmas!" And one of the first years she did this, the year that Taylor was 2 and Levi was 4, Sheri filmed the boys having a little conversation that led to a little physical altercation. Taylor was going to clock Levi with a video game he had in his hand. So Sheri asked, "Taylor, do we hit people with toys or not hit people with toys?"

Now, Taylor has a deep need to be right in life. He's going to be one of those guys who will correct you about stuff like, "Actually, it was the 1963 Cubs, not the '64 Cubs." He has the conviction that if we are going to do it, we have got to get it right, and it has always been there. It is something that many parents would interpret as disrespect, but it's really just Taylor trying to be himself. When we offer choices and share control, people can be themselves because our interactions are respectful. And this video captures Taylor helping Sheri give choices. When she asked, "Do we hit people with toys or not hit people with toys?" Taylor corrected her. He said, "No, no, you say, 'Hit people with *wideos* or not hit people with *wideos*?'" It is hilarious to watch to this day, but it's also a great reminder that little tiny people understand this culture of choice, freedom, and power. They pick up on it and start to do it.

Six or eight months after this incident was filmed, our family went shopping at Mervyn's. At the time, I was a foster care social worker, and I wore a tie every day to work. So, on a birthday or special occasion, we would go shopping and I would get a new shirt and a tie. On this particular occasion, Taylor found a tie rack with all different types of Looney Tunes ties. He came over to me with two ties and said, "Dad, which one you want, this one or this one?" I said, "Hmmm." He said, "You decide or I decide." I said, "Hmm, that one." He put the other one back, and I bought a Looney Tunes tie that day, affirming the practice of raising a powerful 2-year-old through honoring his influence in our relationship.

One day I took Brittney to school. I had a company car and I was usually the only person in it, so the front passenger seat was my desk. I had all my stuff on it. Brittney opened the door, looked at all the stuff, and asked, "Dad, do you want me to sit on your stuff, or do you want to move it?"

"I'll move it."

Making room for people to choose is what builds a culture of honor. When you meet the deep human need in your children to have some control, you communicate to them that their needs matter, that they are valuable. And when you communicate value to your children, they develop a healthy self-concept. But when you establish a way of relating with your children in which they don't have a choice, they learn that the only needs that matter are yours. This leads them to develop a self-concept where they either fight back to get their needs met or they believe their needs don't matter. Then they have to work their way to a healthy perspective where they finally realize, in defiance of all you've taught them, that their needs matter, and so do yours.

We've watched our children go out into the world with a healthy self-concept and demonstrate their ability to assert themselves respectfully. They've also demonstrated their ability to set limits with people, whether they be peers or adults, when they encounter disrespect. Some of the disrespect they have had to deal with has actually been shown by authority figures that have mistaken assertiveness for disrespect. After all, the common belief a generation or so ago was that asserting yourself at all as a child was disrespectful. If that was the attitude in your home growing up and you're trying to give your kids choices, you need to be prepared for them to respond to you in a way that may feel disrespectful. They are going to start picking out Looney Tunes ties for you and telling you to move your stuff out of the seat. They are going to be asserting their will, because they have one. It is our job to make room for this so they can know what it feels like to be respected and that it's right for them to be respected. Obviously it's important that they learn to assert their choices in a respectful way, but they have to be allowed to assert themselves in the first place.

THINK IT OVER

Learning to distinguish assertiveness from disrespect is one important part of cultivating a healthy environment of honor. As you sow respect into your encounters with your children by making room for them to assert themselves, you will reap respect. But there will, no doubt, be incidents where your child is disrespectful, and you need to guide him or her through cleaning up the mess.

So far, some of the messes we have looked at involved disrespect and some didn't. Brittney forgetting her lunchbox wasn't disrespectful. The email example of the little girl throwing a fit to avoid her chores was. But in that case, her mother recognized that her daughter was using disrespect to distract her from enforcing the choice she had put before her. In those cases, as we have seen, you have to be able to stick to your words and not make your child's problem your problem.

As parents, you wear different hats. When you're wearing the IRS hat, you are showing and enforcing the *practical* consequences of your children's choices, and sometimes you must suspend the issue of *relational* consequences. But if your child shows disrespect, it is your job to introduce relational consequences at the earliest appropriate moment, and the first task in both cases is the same. You must guide your child toward taking ownership of the problem.

One of the best ways to do this is to institute something called the *think-it-over chair*. And remember, one of the best ways to get another human being to think it over is by asking them questions and by not finishing your sentences. So when your kid is sitting in the think-it-over chair, your job is to avoid the Charlie Brown schoolteacher lecture mode—"Waa waa waa waa waa"—and create opportunities for your child to think it over by coming up with multiple-choice questions.

Let's consider a situation in which your child shows disrespect to another person. Say that Johnny is your son, and he has just hit the neighbor boy. He is sitting in the think-it-over chair in front of you. You begin by asking, "Johnny, what is the problem?"

He says, "Uh…I don't know. He touched me. He hit me." In other words, Johnny is trying to project that the problem is out there. It's something he can't do anything about. He is a victim. He is powerless. Other people mess up his life.

"Wow, gee. So, you stuck out your tongue and hit him with a stick because of what he said?

"Yeah."

"Wow. Bummer. So, what is the problem here—that he said something or that you did something?"

"Both."

"Well, what can you do about what he says to you?"

"I can hit him!"

"OK. How is that working out for you?"

"I don't know."

"Is hitting Billy respectful or disrespectful?"

"Disrespectful. But he did it first!"

"So just because he was disrespectful means that you have to be disrespectful? Did he make you be disrespectful, or did you choose to be disrespectful?"

"I guess…I chose."

"Is that OK, or is that a problem?"

Remember, your goal in all of this is not to figure out how much blame to assign to each party involved. You are trying to help your son learn that no one can control him but him. You are trying to help him discover that he is a powerful person, but that he will inevitably surrender that power to external forces unless he learns to take responsibility for his choices. Your questions are all designed to lead him to this revelation, and to confront him with the choice: "Are you going to let other people or circumstances or something outside of you control you, or are you going to control you?"

Hopefully as he learns to think it over, to sort through the pile of who said and did what, he will begin to realize, "Oh my gosh, it's right there. It's me. It was my choice to hit Billy with that stick. The problem is that I hit someone, and it was disrespectful." When he starts to identify himself as the owner of the problem, then you can ask, "What are you going to do?"

Here is a portion of a letter I received from a mother who just realized that the problem in her relationship with her daughter was not her daughter's but hers:

[You taught on a CD] about the doctor who discovers he is the problem. Well, we have a grown daughter who lives with us. She has had a drug problem for 9 years. She has been clean for 19 months now. The trouble with it all is she lives with us, along with her two children, and on the weekend we have all three of her kids. That is OK, but she and I are about as opposite as you can get. So therefore we don't always get along. Because of the years of abuse she has handed out, I had gotten very angry and had began to respond in anger a lot. After listening to you, I realized without meaning to I had created a circle of death around us. Opposite of what I wanted to do. I cried when I realized what I had done. Over the next weeks it was rather funny. When I began to react I would say under my breath, "It's you that is the problem!" I thought I was going to have to get duct tape and tape my mouth shut. The Lord began to show me how I had begun to respond to her in anger all the time, and it was the anger that was the problem, not the boundaries I wanted to set. So little by little, as I got me in control I would calmly set the boundaries without anger. A funny thing began to happen; she began to try to please me. (I nearly fell over dead from that one.) Life began to spring up. My husband was gone a whole week, and there wasn't one cross word between her and I. We began to laugh together and even enjoy each other. The best part was on Tuesday. I had to take her to her work, and we went by an old boyfriend's rig. I said, "Is your heart going pitter patter?" She said, "Not anymore. I'm kind of over that." She sighed and I said, "I guess you can't help who you love." She said, "Mom that was the biggest mistake of my life, and it was followed by a whole bunch of bad choices." I started crying. She grabbed my hand and said, "Are you all right"? I said, "Yeah, I just wanted so much more for you than what you have gotten. She said, "I know, but it was my bad choices." We got to where we were going and I said to her, "I really love you, no matter what." She said, "Mom I love you, too." Things have been different between us since the anger is gone.

In your teaching you talked about how we justify our position. Boy howdy, did I have it down good. "It's me!" has been really good for me. I hope to have this down soon. I listened to another CD again this morning on the way to work. That makes 14 times…. I'm sure I'll get it soon.

Thank you for putting these tools out there for us to use. It really helps those of us who want to produce something different, a way to look at their circumstance and say, you know, this problem just might be mine. As God changes me, we get to see the world around us change to that which we wanted in the first place.

Hundreds of reports just like this one have come in over the years.

DISCIPLINE OR PUNISHMENT?

It's exciting when your child (or you, the parent) reaches the point where he or she identifies and owns the problem, because when the problem has an owner, it can be fixed. This is the point where true discipline can begin. The difference

---

between punishment and discipline is a powerful child. The child is involved in making decisions about how to clean up the mess. Punishment is when the adult makes all the decisions in the situation. "This is what's going to happen, young man. You are going to be grounded for two weeks and then you're going to mow the lawn every week and then you're going to apologize to those people and then you're going to take the paint off the wall..." The nature of punishment is control, and the spirit behind it is fear. But perfect love drives out all fear, fear has to do with punishment, and you've not been given a spirit of fear but of power, love, and self-control (1 John 4:18; 2 Tim. 1:7).

I would like to talk about the practice of spanking at this point. Many parents find themselves confused at the separation of fear and spanking. I will tell you a story of a time when Levi received a spanking and as a goal, was empowered throughout the entire incident.

One January evening, Sheri and I were out with friends. Brittney was watching both their children and ours. Upon returning to the house, we discovered a completely frustrated older sister who had many complaints about her younger brother's behavior for the night. As I investigated the evening, I learned that the moment Britt announced it was time to go to bed, about 11:00 P.M., Levi, who was about 8 years old at the time, promptly ran outside into the freezing night air and stayed outside for over half an hour while his sister tried to "yellow truck" him into the house.

Once we arrived home, I asked Levi to come into the living room with me. I mentioned to him that I heard from his sister that they had a rough night together. He agreed. I then began to look into his eyes and led him through his discipline.

"Son," I began, "There is a spirit that is after you, and it's called, 'Rebellion.' It sounds like this, 'Don't do what the authority in your life is telling you to do.' Have you heard this voice before?"

"Yes," he said.

"Ah, I thought so. Son, it is your job to chase that voice away. It is very important that you do not let that spirit lead you. Tonight...I am going to help you." And I brought him around in front of me and bent him over my lap. He had the most puzzled look on his face. *Whap*! A swift, firm hand to the buttocks landed.

"Yelp!"

I asked quietly, about three inches from his left ear. "Is it gone?"

Lips pursed and rubbing the hotspot on his left butt cheek, he answered, "*Yes!*"

"All right, son. If you ever need my help again, just let me know. I love you."

What is the difference here and most occasions involving a spanking? Here we have an empowered child. At every step of the process, Levi had a powerful role. He was thinking, learning, and deciding through each question I asked. He emerged from this discipline an educated young man. Too many incidents of spanking turn into punishment. By this I mean the child has no choice but to endure the process of the parent's power. Often, an offended parent is issuing the pronounced sentence of "You lied, you get a spanking. You did what I said not to, you get a spanking. You hit your sister, you get a spanking," and so on.

Probably the key difference between discipline and punishment is anger. Discipline has much to do with the presence of a *disciple*. This essentially means "a learner." Now, I know many of us have been told, "I am going to teach you a lesson. Now, pull down your pants. This is going to hurt me more than it is going to hurt you." That's not the "learning" I am talking about.

Let me get back to my point about learners. Discipline brings forth a certain virtue in the one being taught. It is important to see that discipline has different results, depending on the one bringing the "disciple" along in training. Discipline brings to the surface the very best that resides within the teacher. For example, if the teacher has a powerful anointing in prayer and intercession, then the student will learn to cry out for revival, declare things to the heavens, fast for weeks at a time, and believe for global justice in our generation. All of these virtues flow from the teacher to the disciple. But if the teacher has a strong leadership anointing, then the student will learn to develop an internal leadership paradigm, be ready to "give up in order to move up," and cultivate a strong "inner circle" of leader influences in their lives. Again, these different *disciplines* flow from the teacher's life into the life of the student. *Therefore, discipline is all about me reaching into your life and pulling the best of me to the surface in you.*

Punishment has an entirely different goal. In punishment, the goal is to introduce a false belief. The belief is that sin must be punished. Whenever someone breaks the rules, the introduction of pain and suffering is required. People are afraid of other people who break rules. This fear is most often manifested in anger. Remember that anger is a false sense of power—power to control others.

This model, too, has a learner, but this learner must understand penitence. There must be a demonstration of sorrow for sin. "Say you're sorry," is a common response to our child's mistake. We, as parents, often think that saying "sorry" means sorrow. It doesn't, but it remains a necessary performance nonetheless. This show of sorrow, once reached, opens the door for the punisher to enter, because having pain and suffering inflicted upon me makes more sense if I'm sorry for sin.

Punishment, obviously, has a punisher. As I discussed earlier, this relationship presents a model where one person has all the power and control and the other person has none. The punisher is allowed to do most anything he or she wants while punishing the other person. Laws have to be created to reign in the punisher's freedoms over the person being punished. I know this all sounds crazy, but think about the goal of torture. It is to gain a confession. And a confession, in turn, allows the punisher to do his job with a sense of righteousness and justice. This external approach to correction requires that both parties believe that people can control each other.

Discipline works from the inside out, and punishment tries to work from the outside in. The parent who comes alongside to discipline is going to manifest these core beliefs and practices. The parent who is bringing learning to a student is not going to try to control the child, but is skillfully going to invite the child to own and solve his own problem.

THE POWER OF QUESTIONS

Asking a good question is a far more powerful tool in leading children to a solution than telling them what you think. That is why you ask questions—to involve their participation in the solution. Then the solution will be amazing because it is something *the child created*: his or her answer to your question. It is precisely this involvement in creating solutions that teaches your children the important truths you want them to learn.

I remember a time when Levi had hurt his brother, Taylor, again. They were still young, around 9 and 11 years old. I heard about the altercation and called my son in from playing in the yard. I confronted him with a series of questions in hopes of leading him to a solution.

"Son, how you doing?"

"Fine."

"Awesome. Hey, I was wondering why you punched your brother?"

"I don't know."

"Ok, well, how about you sit right here until you know. I'll be right over there if you need any help figuring this out. Let me know, OK?"

"He's always being mean to me!" he blurted out. See, he'd been in that chair before. He knew that he was in charge of how long he stayed there. He wanted to get through it as quickly as possible.

"Oh, no. He's being mean to you? How is he being mean to you?"

"He doesn't want me to play with him and his friends." He began to cry.

"Oh, no. You sound like that is hurting your heart."

"I hate it, and I hate him!"

"Ah, you are hating your brother. How is that working out for you?"

"Well, he doesn't care. He doesn't love me!" He was really crying by this point.

"Buddy, this is a big hurt in your heart, isn't it?"

"Yes."

"What are you going to do?"

"Say sorry?"

"Ah, say sorry. Hmm, do you think Taylor will believe you if you say 'sorry' to him?"

"Uh, I think so."

"Okay, well let's try it." I called Taylor in from his playing and informed him that his brother had something he'd like to say. Taylor stood with a guarded posture, arms folded, in front of Levi.

Levi looked at Taylor with a tear-stained face and said, "Sorry."

I then turned to Taylor and asked, "Do you believe him when he says 'sorry'?"

Taylor said, "No! I think he is just trying to not be in trouble anymore."

"Ahhh," I said. "Tay, thanks for coming in. See you later." He ran off to play.

I then turned to Levi and said, "Dang, that didn't seem to work. What are you going to do now?"

"I don't know!" He was almost distraught. "What can I do if he doesn't believe me when I say 'sorry'?"

"Great question, son. Why doesn't Taylor believe you when you say you are sorry?"

"I don't know."

"Do you need some time to think it over?"

"No, but I don't know what to do."

"Do you mind if I ask you some more questions?"

"No."

"OK, you told me that Taylor had done some things that hurt your heart. Like, he wasn't letting you join in with him and his friends. Is that right?"

"Yes."

"Did you ever forgive your brother for hurting you?"

"No."

"Do you think that this may be why you keep hurting him, because even though this happened a while ago, it feels like he is still hurting you?"

"Yeah."

"What are you going to do, son?"

"Forgive Taylor."

"Ah, how do you think that will work out for you?"

"Better."

"Cool. Is that something you want to by yourself or do you want my help?"

"Your help."

"OK, well, how do you think Jesus is feeling knowing that you are hurting your brother, sad or glad?"

"Sad."

"Do you want to clean this up with Jesus, too?"

"Yeah."

"OK, well, repeat after me." And I led him through a prayer of repentance and forgiveness. I then asked him, "How's that feel?"

"Way better."

"What you going to do now?"

"I think I want to ask Taylor again to forgive me. I think he'll believe me this time because I really am sorry now."

"Awesome! I'll go get him."

And sure enough, Levi was right. Taylor believed him this time because he was ready to clean up his mess with his brother. The power of good questions is in the pathway they create for your child to find the solution and carry it out.

Remember, you want your children to learn three primary things from their mistakes. First, you want them to learn that choices on the outside can create hurt on the inside. The hurt might be connected to the fact that they hurt you, to something they lost, or to something they experienced. But it is happening on the *inside,* and that pain is what will motivate them to change their behavior in the future. Second, you want them to learn that they are capable of creating solutions to their own problems. And third, you want them to learn that their parents are sources of wisdom and help that are always available for them as they go about creating those solutions.

With these goals in mind, your job is to send him three of the important messages we have discussed throughout the book. First, you want your child to know that you are sad for him because he has a problem. Remember, you cannot force your child to feel sorry when he makes a mistake. What you can show him is that *you are sorry*, because you love him and you know that the consequences of his poor choice will probably be painful. "Bummer." Second, you want your child to know that you believe in his or her ability to figure out what to do and to do it. "Buddy, you're pretty smart, and I know you want to do the right thing. You're going to get through this." And third, you want your child to know that you are happy and willing to help him figure out what to do. "Don't know what to do? Well, I have some suggestions for you if you would like to hear them." As soon as he asks, "What?" his little heart opens up. The little shield that covers his heart from all wisdom ever affecting it comes off. Then wisdom gets in there, and you get to be a part of his decision. That "What?" is music to your ears. At that point, you get to feed the hungry. Blessed are those who hunger and thirst for righteousness, for they will be filled

(Matt. 5:6). And, "...any man who lacks wisdom should *ask* God who is generous..." (James 1:5).

CLEANING UP OUR MESSES

The right answer can only come with the right question, which is, "What are you going to do?" If your child is truly sorry, she'll clean up her mess. But she can only get there if you have a paradigm in which you expect her to be able to find the problem and take responsibility for it. So many people don't expect that from others. They expect that when you make a mess, it is theirs to clean up, and they have to order you through the steps to clean up the mess. They need control of you in the problem. Your job is to comply or rebel. But nothing on the inside ever changes. It's a paradigm of external control.

It can be scary to do this with your children, because it's vulnerable. You are taking the risk of revealing your heart, and you can't control what they are going to do. But it is so vital that you do this, because this is probably the most profound way in which your children learn just how powerful they are. Their choices have the power to hurt the people they love most. And if they don't learn this at a young age, then they will have no clue about cleaning up their messes in adulthood. It is a much tougher lesson to learn when we get older, but it can be done.

I work with many adults in relationships and marriages who don't know what to do when they make a mess. When someone sends them the message, "You said that. It hurts me," they don't know how to respond. So they say things like, "Well, it shouldn't.

You're too sensitive." That's always helpful, huh? Not really. In fact, it creates a scenario much like the following.

Imagine that you have a puppy running around the house and he has an accident on the living room floor. You grab the puppy, swat him with a rolled-up newspaper, and throw him outside. Ah, problem solved, right? If the goal was punishing the mistake, then it is solved. But what is the real problem here? The mess on the floor is the biggest problem! Can you imagine being satisfied with punishing the dog and leaving the mess there? "Let's just wait for it to set up and it won't track. It's worse when it's fresh. It will calm down. We can put a chair over the top of it so no one steps in it." How long would you live like this? How many messes can a dog make in its lifetime?

Of course, you wouldn't do that, right? You would be running around right away cleaning it up. Yet too many households operate like this. When people make disrespectful messes in their relationships, they so often just let these messes fester and fill their home environment. It isn't too long before they can't go anywhere without stepping in something. The years fill it up. Husbands and wives come to bed and it's all over the bed. It's everywhere—messes everywhere. And it seems that all people know to do is to continue figuring out creative ways to deny the messes. "What? Are you still bringing that up?" It becomes normal to live in an environment that is filled with disrespectful messes that nobody has taken responsibility to address. The issue of breaking the rules is addressed with punishment, but the condition of broken hearts and connections is left alone.

The point is that avoiding messes like that is something we learn in childhood. This lesson teaches us to value avoiding punishment more than maintaining a relationship connection. So, the interaction in the think-it-over chair is pretty important. This is where they get to discover what the problem is, how it has affected or is going to affect the quality of their life and relationships, and gain the tools they need to make things right and restore their connection with those they love most. This healthy confrontation, as much as all the other ways you demonstrate your love to children, has the power to build your connection with them and establish the priority of relationship in their hearts.

HOUSTON, WE HAVE A PROBLEM

Do you remember the movie *Apollo 13*? It's the story of a NASA program where a bunch of things went wrong with the spacecraft while the astronauts were headed for the moon. There is a scene toward the end of the movie where Houston had to help them figure out what the problem was with a scrubber that wasn't taking the carbon dioxide out of their breathing air. They then had to give instructions to the astronauts, who had to decipher them and try to repair the vehicle with the parts they had on board. Their next big concern was whether the command module, *Odyssey,* could survive reentering Earth's atmosphere because earlier there had been an explosion while mixing the oxygen tanks. That explosion damaged their heat shield. A successful reentry came down to several things—the strength of the heat shield and the *Odyssey.* A typhoon was building in the landing area and the parachutes might not open upon command. Also, as the vehicle reentered, there would be three minutes where they completely lost communication. After that time, Houston would know if they had made it alive.

I think this is a very compelling parenting analogy. You see, these wonderful people who are growing up in your home, who you love so much, are going to go through a period called adolescence. And in that period, things will happen inside of them that they don't understand. They are going to change right before your very eyes as they try to find the handle on this thing called life. These changes can make for some scary moments as you parent an adolescent. There are times when it feels like, "I cannot communicate with you. I cannot reach you. I don't know where you went. I am afraid of what is happening to you during this time." You, the parents, are Houston trying to send messages to your teenagers, *Apollo 13*, so they can find a way to put things together and come through the journey of figuring things out intact.

It is the relationship we have with our children, in essence, that helps them to keep their heat shield and control module strong. When hormones and peer pressure and culture are raging against your adolescents, they need the protection of being connected to your heart. If your relationship with them has been damaged, it's going to be tough for them to withstand the external and internal pressures they are facing. This is why it is so important that when scary things happen with your adolescents, you know how to make sure that love drives out fear and your connection stays strong.

When Brittney was 16 years old, something happened that we thought would never happen. We disconnected. It was during a time when our family was moving from one town to another, and all of us were "disconnecting" from our friends and waiting to build new relationships where we were going. Sheri and I did not see what was coming.

It was October 2001. We'd moved to Redding from Weaverville. We were the new Family Life pastors of Bethel Church. We had resigned our position as senior pastors at Mountain Chapel in Weaverville. Life was filled with change, and all the strange emotions that come with a move. But for the most part, life seemed pretty much normal.

I arrived home one Saturday night after a long day working with domestic violence offenders in Weaverville. I now had about an hour drive home from work, so I didn't pull into the driveway until about 8:00 P.M. Both boys came running out to meet me. They began telling me, "Dad! Mom is on the floor crying! Come in the house quick. Brittney is missing!" I couldn't make sense of what they were telling me. As I entered the house, there on the kitchen floor was my bride. She was curled up in the fetal position, sobbing. I went down on the floor to ask her what was wrong. She tried to utter, "Brittney is missing." Even after she told me, I couldn't make sense of what that meant. She got up off the floor and began to tell me the story.

Around 9:00 A.M. Britt was preparing for her day. She was going over to a friend's house that she hadn't seen in several years. It was exciting for Sheri to see her reconnect with an old friend. She left the house shortly thereafter and said she'd be home around noon. Britt had her own car, a cell phone, a job, and all the trust in the world when she walked out that door.

Sheri tried to reach her about 11:00 A.M. to find out what her lunch plans were for the day. She left a couple messages on the cell phone, but Britt didn't return any of the messages. The phone was new to Britt and it was unusual for her not to answer, let alone not to return a call. So, Sheri called the home of the friend. "She never showed," said the friend. Sheri was stunned, then confused, and then began to be filled with fear about what was going on.

She called as many places as she knew to call, trying to find someone who knew where Britt was. Nothing. No one knew where she was. It was a new environment. There weren't very many places she would be. What was going on?

Finally, she thought to call a cousin in southern California. We'd just traveled south for a vacation and we'd spent some time with family. Maybe Jake knew something. Sheri asked him if he had any idea where she might be. He paused long enough for Sheri to think he knew something. "If you know where she is you'd better tell me right now!" she said, revving her yellow truck.

"She met someone on the Internet this last summer. She is going to meet him at the park today for the first time in person," he told her.

She went cold upon hearing this news. "Thanks, Jake." She hung up the phone. This had really become a parent's worst nightmare. Brittney was meeting someone she met on the Internet. There were 20 parks in Redding. She had been missing for three hours. She had just introduced fear into her relationship with Sheri like never before.

I was out of town and out of cell phone range all day. Brittney and I had both of our family's cars. We were in a new town at a new church. We knew no one. Sheri was in a panic. We did have some friends who could help: Kris and Kathy Vallotton. She called Kris and explained the situation. While she was talking to him, he turned to Kathy and said, "Pray, this is serious." She hung up the phone and did all that she could—wait. Wait until I get home.

After I heard this story, I called the police. The officer began taking my information. As I described my daughter and her car to the police, it all began to sink in. This was really happening. Brittney was missing. It had been since 9 A.M. and it was now after 8 P.M., about eleven hours at this point. While I was on the phone with the police, Sheri's cell phone rang. It was Kathy Vallotton. She said, "Kris asked the Lord where we should go and He told him to go to a certain park. When we arrived, there she was, standing there with a boy. A 17-year-old boy. Kris went over to them and told Britt to get into the car with me. He is going to stay and talk to this boy. I have her with me, and we are on our way to your house. See you in a few minutes."

We were so relieved that she was alive and then suddenly we were both furious! The internal conversation was, "OK, she's safe! Now we are going to kill her!" We were dripping with fear. And people who are afraid want control. Yep, that was us. We so desperately wanted to control this child so she would not scare us like this ever again. *No fun!*

She entered the house with Kathy in tow. Britt's face was red, and she looked mad. I pointed to the living room, and she went in and sat down. We thanked Kathy, and she left. Brittney was not repentant or sorry. She was angry and defensive, and her demeanor confused me. This was not typical for her.

We had two options. We could show her our anger, or we could show her what was really going on, and that was a broken heart. I remembered giving this advice to a friend who had had a similar situation with his teenage daughter. I didn't remember it being as hard to give that advice as I was finding it hard to follow. I was scared and hurt like never before. I felt vulnerable and confused. So, that's where we started.

Sheri did a great job sitting in silence during this whole process. She knew that it was the best choice after a day like she had had. She watched most of the time, interjecting from time to time. I moved in close to Britt and began to tell her that I was scared and hurt. Thankfully, we knew that when someone does something that scares us or hurts us, it is a mistake to show anger in an effort to feel powerful. A human being's response to another person's anger is very different than a response to a person's hurt or fear. So we chose B and spent an evening showing her our broken hearts. We did that because we knew we wanted connection with her and she needed to know that whatever was going on with her had stepped right into the middle of our hearts.

When I asked her to help me understand how we got "here," her response was something like this: "Mom and Dad, I'm a Christian because you're a Christian. I'm a Christian because I'm a pastor's daughter. All my friends are Christians. I've gone to a Christian school. Everybody we know is a Christian. I'm a Christian because everybody I know is. I want to find out what else there is. This book," she said, pointing to the Bible, "is a bunch of stories to me."

I braced myself for what was coming next.

"I don't want to be a Christian anymore. I want to do things that other teenagers do. I don't know what is wrong with that. And I know that it's not something you are going to let me do." She went on to say, "You have no idea how much pressure I live under being your daughter. Everyone thinks I am supposed to be perfect. Well, I am not! And I don't think I should have to live like I am!"

Up until that moment, I had thought that was the worst night of my life. But after she opened that can, I wasn't sure how we were going to recover. It was as if the floor had disappeared and I was falling through black space. I did not know what to do. All my years of giving parents advice somehow left me. I sat there in silence and prayed my all-time favorite prayer, "Jesus, Jesus, Jesus, Jesus, Jesus, Jesus!"

I couldn't remember much, but I could remember that I must fight to stay connected to my child's heart. And fight I would. I moved closer to the one who was scaring me and hurting more than anyone ever had. I sat at her feet and told her, "Britt, I had no idea that you had any of this going on inside. I am sorry. I should have paid closer attention. I had no idea that you were feeling all this pressure. But here's what you've got to understand. I have one real priority in my life. That is to make sure that you, your brothers, your mom, and I all end up on the other side together when this is all said and done. So, if I am doing something to injure our connection or if what I do for a living is putting too much pressure on you, then I am done. Tomorrow I will go find another job. I can find work anywhere. And that's that. I love you, and I am sorry that I missed all this."

We all went to bed late that Saturday night. The next morning, as you may have guessed, was Sunday, and I had to go to work. I had duties to perform. We had come to be the family life pastors at Bethel Church and had just been there a month. We were there to show families how to do life, and we had been telling people how to do it for years. Now, suddenly, we were faced with the question of how we were going to do it, in a situation we had never encountered and that was completely out of our control.

Praise God I wasn't preaching that morning, because by the time we got to the middle of worship, I couldn't take it anymore. Brittney had stayed home, and I left the service and went home to be with her. She was sitting on the couch watching some sad, make-you-cry girl movie, and I just came and sat down next her. I put her legs over my legs and sat there and didn't say a word. She didn't say a word. I didn't really know what to do except to do my best to convince her that I loved her so much and being connected to her was my top priority.

Even though we were scared, we knew that it was time that Brittney, who had been serving her parents' God, found hers. It is no easy task to let go of your child and say, "Find Him." Days seemed like years and weeks seemed like decades. She didn't go to church. She didn't do a bunch of things that we would have liked to see her do. But she was not disrespectful, she didn't push us away, and she was not punished. We tried to stay connected through the toughest thing we had ever been through. And in the end, we were blessed. After four months of figuring things out, she made a decision to follow the Lord. There was even a fairytale ending—Ben came from Australia, rode in on his white pony, swooped her up, and they are living happily ever after. But it was the scariest time of our lives.

I share this story in order to show you that there are no guarantees. I'm sure you know that. Sheri and I don't have some storybook deal going on here. Just like you, we are working our heads off trying to stay connected to these little people we love so much, who have their own choices to make. That is why it is so critical that you understand what your parenting goal is and develop the tools to reach it. The goal isn't to get them to clean their room; it is to strengthen the connection to your heart. We will deal with the room, but if we lose the connection, we've lost the big stuff. We may win the battle, but we've lost the war. We have to learn how to stay connected to their hearts while we teach them to think, to problem solve, to be responsible, to be respectful, to be loving. And you can only stay connected to their hearts when you know how to get connected and how to protect that connection.

GUIDED BY YOUR EYE

I also share this story because I know that one of your greatest desires as a Christian parent is to lead your children successfully into a relationship with God. Fumbling this goal is probably one of the greatest fears we parents have. It is my conviction that the tools I have been presenting in this book are keys to achieving this goal because they are ways of relating that derive directly from the way that God relates to us in the New Covenant. As I have said, I believe that the closer we get to loving our children like God does, the more readily and easily they will step toward loving Him.

Remember, in the New Covenant we are governed internally by exercising self-control. But self-control is driven by your values, by what is important to you. A lot of people think of self-control as the ability to say no to bad things. But I believe that self-control is much more positive. I define it as the ability to say yes to something so completely that all other options are eliminated—including things that aren't necessarily bad in themselves but that would distract you from pursuing the thing that is most important and valuable to you. People of self-control have identified their top priority, and their value for that thing motivates them to pursue it to the exclusion of everything else.

There are plenty of athletes, business owners, professionals, artists, and entertainers in our society who exercise extraordinary levels of discipline in order to achieve their goals. But every believer has been called to something far different and greater than mere achievement. We have been called to be sons and daughters of God. Our first identity and priority is found in our restored, intimate relationship with our Father. It is through this intimacy that we are to bear fruit and mature into sons who look just like Jesus. It is through this intimacy that we bear the fruit of self-control. The more deeply we come to know our Father, the more our internal value for our connection with God grows, and it is this value that motivates us to embrace a lifestyle that will build and protect that connection.

I want to review what Psalm 32:8-9 says about the way that God intends for His connection with us to direct us:

> *I will instruct you and teach you in the way you should go.* **I will guide you with my eye.** *Do not be like the horse or like the mule, which have no understanding, which must be harnessed with bit and bridle, else they will not come near you.*

The second part of the verse is pretty easy to understand. The horse and mule require an external source of control to direct them. God doesn't want us to be controlled externally, but instead, He wants us to be led by His *eye*. Now, think about that for a minute. Has an eyeball ever slapped you around? No. So how does the Lord direct us with His eye? The eyes are the windows of the heart. God directs us by letting us know how our choices affect His heart. When we make choices that violate our connection with him and violate who we are, the Holy Spirit convicts us, which is basically a message that says, "Hey, look into Daddy's eyes. Do you see that what you are doing breaks His heart?" Unfortunately, if we are still thinking like mules, we mistake the conviction of the Holy Spirit to mean, "Oh, God's getting mad. He is about to smite your hind parts if you don't straighten up and fly right." But that's not at all what conviction is. Ephesians 4:30 says, "Do not grieve the Holy Spirit of God." Our sins hurt His heart. And when we hurt His heart, He invites us to look into His eyes and see that. He trusts us with His heart, and trusts that the concern that we have for His heart will direct us.

This is the same kind of relationship I have tried to cultivate with my children. A few years ago, I came home from a trip and I noticed that the lawn had not been mowed. It happened to be during summer vacation, when mowing the lawn was Levi's job. I asked him, "Hey buddy, do you see that lawn?"

He said, "Yeah, yeah."

I asked, "What do you think?"

"Yeah, it needs to be mowed."

I said, "Ah, cool. So when were you going to do that?"

"Well, uh…tomorrow?"

I said, "Tomorrow's perfect. Awesome. Cool."

I came home the next day and the lawn wasn't mowed and he was away doing whatever. He came home and I said, "Hey, buddy, I came home today and the lawn wasn't mowed."

He said, "I forgot."

I said, "Yeah, I know. So would you like for me to forget that you have some things that I need to buy for football?"

"No."

"Okay, so how do you think I feel when you forget to take care of something that is important to me and that you told me you were going to do? How do you think I feel?"

He said, "Not good. Hurt. I'm sorry."

"What are you going to do?"

"I'll mow that lawn."

"When?"

"In the morning."

I said, "That will do."

He said, "Dad, I am sorry."

I said, "I forgive you."

The lawn was mowed by the time I got home. I think he even did it in the morning. No yelling, threats, or allowances were involved. There was no attitude like, "I can't believe this. You have all day. I work; you don't. I am amazing; you are a bum." He simply looked in my eyes and saw my heart, and that matters to him because we are connected at the heart. I can guide my son with my eye because I trust him. I trust that Levi cares about my heart, and so I am going to show it to him. The concern that Levi has for my heart directs him.

If he didn't care about my heart, then he wouldn't have cared that I had just showed it to him. And if he didn't care about my heart, then the lawn wouldn't matter. Your only hope to influence your teenager is a heart connection. You cannot govern a teenager with rules. You can govern little ones with rules, but when kids begin to grow up, your influence will be determined by their value for their relationship with you. If power struggles have damaged your connection, then they probably won't really care how their choices affect you.

Raising a teenager is like flying a kite on a windy day. Teens are blown around by culture, by peer pressure, and by hormones, and the string is my connection to my teenager, from my heart to his heart. And if that string is all torn up by power struggles and disrespect, that force against it will be too strong. It won't be too long before *snap* goes the string, and there goes my child, blown by the forces of this world. And the one who wants to influence him the most, the one who loves him the most, the one who has these jewels of wisdom to add to his life, is cut off. We want to learn to strengthen our kids' heart connections to us so that we can steer them with our eyes. When they look in our eyes, they will know, "Oh, what I am doing is affecting your heart. It's hurting you. I am sorry." They direct themselves to honor us. This is governing from the inside out.

TRUE SUBMISSION

Submission is a sign of a love connection. It has nothing to do with external pressure. True submission says, "I direct myself to honor you and to empower you in my life. I choose to stay connected to you." I believe that true submission is the key to becoming all that we can be. One of the reasons that God has done so much to protect our freedom is that we can only become the people He created us to be through willing submission to what is important to Him. It's called faith. We may not understand His reasons for asking us to do a particular thing, but because we have a loving connection with Him, we trust Him and we submit to doing it because it's important to Him. This is what He meant when He said, "If you love me, keep my commandments" (John 14:15). True obedience can only flow from love. This obedience is what brings out the gold in us.

Likewise, I believe that without true submission and obedience that flows from a loving connection with us, our children won't really be able to grow and develop the potential that we see and desire to draw out of them.

A few years ago, Levi failed half of his first round of standardized testing in high school. His school counselor had notified us that he was going to have to retake one of the tests. He'd missed a passing score by one point.

As the date moved closer to us, I asked him if he was studying for the upcoming test.

He said, "It's stupid. I don't care about how I do on this test. Last time I just made designs out of the bubbles on the scan-tron sheet."

"Wow!" I thought to myself, "...and you only missed it by one? Hmm?" But out loud I said, "Buddy, hey, here's the deal. I think you believe that this is a measure of your intelligence. It's not. It's a measurement of your willingness to try. I know this is no fun, but it's very important to me that you are willing to try. I don't care how you do on this test. You know what? I'll bet you don't know anybody, not even your principal, who can tell you one of his or her scores on this test. Do you know your score from last year? Do you know Taylor's score? I don't know any of mine. Nobody knows. It's a big secret. They keep it at the Wizard of Oz's place. Unless you're a genius, nobody cares. But what does matter is whether you try when things are hard. This is such an important life lesson that you walk toward things that scare you sometimes. It is part of becoming a man that you don't let failure control your life. That is a lesson I need you to learn. That's important to me. What are you going to do?"

He says, "I hate it when you say that."

"Probably so."

"I don't know what I am going to do, Dad."

I said, "Well, when you figure it out, I need you to go talk to your counselor and let her know what you're going to do."

He went back to retake the test. The next section he had to take was math, his worst subject. Afterward he told me, "You know, I looked at every single problem and I didn't know most of them. But I tried on every single one."

"How do you think you did?" I asked.

"I don't know, but I tried this time."

"How does that make you feel?"

"Better. Better than just making designs out of the bubbles."

His heart is tied to my heart, and my heart is tied to his heart. That is really all I care about. I don't care about his test scores. I care about whether he is going to try hard, no matter how big the mountain gets in his life. That's what I care about. If I know that he can do that, and if he knows he can do that, then I know he's going to be fine. I can ask him to respond to what I care about before he understands it because we have a relationship of trust, love, respect, and honor.

Obviously we must have had a relationship to be able to do that, because otherwise, it would be perceived as angry punishment. But when you do have a relationship, you can let the person see your heart through your actions as well as your words. Personally, I think it's best if you can simply say, "You know what? It hurts my heart to see you not trying very hard. I know you can do better." But use wisdom to recognize when more is needed than words.

PREVENTING PROBLEMS

In closing, I want to point out that it may be easy for you to read this chapter and think that maintaining a loving connection with your child is all about confrontation and the think-it-over chair. Many people don't know how to do this well, so it's worth learning. But as we as a society are learning in the area of health, the best way to live is to think preventatively, to embrace a lifestyle of health that will create an environment where problems just don't tend to happen very often. When problems do occur, a healthy person can bounce back from them a lot better and faster.

The only way that many of these tools for fixing problems can work is if you as parents have already made your family relationships your priority and are investing your time and energy into those relationships. They can only work if you are proactively creating an environment of love in your home through your words and actions. Most of us are familiar with the simple things that help to build relationship—serving one another, laughing together, talking, collaborating, encouraging and comforting each other. As believers, we also have the privilege and responsibility to recognize and call out the divine destiny in one another. When you build up and delight in one another in these ways, you are causing the value of your relationship to increase. And it is this value, the value that comes from enjoying and serving one another, that will clarify the choices that your children will be led to make when there's a problem.

My final exhortation to you is that you continually be seeking ways to grow as proactive, extravagant lovers in your home. Love on purpose, just as God does:

Watch what God does, and then you do it, like children who learn proper behavior from their parents. Mostly what God does is love you. Keep company with him and learn a life of love. Observe how Christ loved us. His love was not cautious but extravagant. He didn't love in order to get something from us but to give everything of himself to us. Love like that (Ephesians 5:1-2 TM).

FINAL POINTS TO PONDER:

1. Do you make room for your children to assert their wills and influence your decisions in an appropriate way?

2. Have you tried using shame and commands to guide your children toward feeling remorse for their mistakes? Why is it harder but more effective to show them a broken heart?

3. Are you a person who needs to be the one with the answers all the time? What must you do to suspend your need to be right when it comes to allowing your children to discover his/her problem and come up with a solution for it?

4. Why is it so vital that you communicate your faith in your child in the midst of his/her failure?

5. What is the difference between punishing people for making a mess and actually cleaning up the mess?

6. What are some things that you desire for your children to grow in that they will only step into through their heart-to-heart connection with you?

Ministry Resources

Loving Our Kids on Purpose Video and Audio Training Sessions and Workbook

Please visit: www.LovingOnPurpose.com

Here is a fresh look at the age-old role of parenting. *Loving Our Kids on Purpose* brings the principles of the Kingdom of God and revival into our strategy as parents. This six-hour training set is available in both DVD and CD. It also has a companion workbook for classroom and small-group training.

Defining the Relationship: A Premarital Course for Those Considering Marriage

Please visit: www.LovingOnPurpose.com

Within this nine-session series, you will find Danny's comedic style of presenting as well as a serious reality check for couples to consider when moving toward marriage discussions. The goal of this series is to impart *courage*—courage to either push through the challenging realities of the relationship or the courage to walk away from the relationship.

RECOMMENDED READING

A Life of Miracles by Bill Johnson

Basic Training for the Prophetic Ministry by Kris Vallotton

Basic Training for the Supernatural Ways of Royalty by Kris Vallotton

Developing a Supernatural Lifestyle by Kris Vallotton

Dreaming With God by Bill Johnson

Face to Face by Bill Johnson

Here Comes Heaven by Mike Seth and Bill Johnson

Parenting with Love and Logic by Foster Cline, M.D. and Jim Fay

Purity by Kris Vallotton

Strengthen Yourself in the Lord by Bill Johnson

The Supernatural Power of a Transformed Mind by Bill Johnson

The Supernatural Ways of Royalty by Kris Vallotton and Bill Johnson

The Ultimate Treasure Hunt by Kevin Dedmon

When Heaven Invades Earth by Bill Johnson

IN THE RIGHT HANDS THIS BOOK WILL CHANGE LIVES!

Most of the people that need this message will not be looking for this book. To change their life you need to put a copy of this book in their hands.

> *But others (seeds) fell into good ground, and brought forth fruit, some a hundred-fold, some sixty-fold, some thirty-fold* (Matthew 13:3-8).

Our ministry is constantly seeking methods to find the good ground, the people that need this anointed message to change their life. Will you help us reach these people?

> *Remember this—a farmer who plants only a few seeds will get a small crop. But the one who plants generously will get a generous crop* (2 Corinthians 9:6).

EXTEND THIS MINISTRY BY SOWING
3-BOOKS, 5-BOOKS, 10-BOOKS, **OR MORE TODAY,**
AND BECOME A LIFE CHANGER!

Thank you,

Don Nori Sr., Publisher
Destiny Image
Since 1982